Praise for *Why Can't I Just Be Me?*

"I have read a lot of books on leadership, business, and personal growth. This one tops them all. *Why Can't I Just Be Me?* is a heartfelt and inspiring read that invites you on a transformative journey towards self-acceptance and authentic leadership. Through personal stories and practical guidance, Melissa sheds light on the challenges of conforming to societal expectations, and encourages readers to accept and embrace who they really are. This is a book that will truly inspire you to embrace your uniqueness and make an impact on the world by being YOU."

— Tarek Riman
CEO of Riman Agency, professor at
Concordia, McGill, and York Universities

"This book is a true demonstration of Melissa's broad experience and impressive talent to unlock what people need to put forward in their lives in order to set fundamental grounds of balance and harmony. Her core lessons, meaningful guidelines, and inspiring reflection tips are life changing and can truly guide anyone to thrive in an enlightening and fulfilling professional and personal path."

— Stephanie David CPA-MBA
director of finance, mother-of-two trying her best

"*Why Can't I Just Be Me?* is more than just a book; it's an empowering journey towards self-discovery and authenticity. Melissa, in her outstanding approach, delicately guides readers through the deepest recesses of their hearts and minds, illuminating forgotten spaces within themselves. Melissa's knack for instilling wisdom within every page of this transformative manual is second to none!"

— Jonathan Defoy
founder and CEO of FoodHero

"Melissa Dawn is the epitome of continual personal growth. Allow this book to take you on an exciting journey of self-discovery!"

— Lydia Aboulian
founder of Mouvement Lavallois,
animal welfare advocate

Why Can't I Just Be Me?

REMOVE THE MASKS THAT HIDE YOU FROM THE WORLD AND FROM YOURSELF

MELISSA DAWN

Brandylane
Publishers, Inc.
Publishing books since 1985

ISBN: 978-1-958754-60-3
Library of Congress Control Number: 2023913102

Designed by Sami Langston
Project managed by Grace Albritton

Printed in the United States of America

Published by
Brandylane Publishers, Inc.
5 S. 1st Street
Richmond, Virginia 23219

Brandylane
Publishers, Inc.
Publishing books since 1985

brandylanepublishers.com

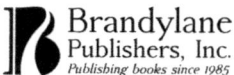

This book is dedicated to people I hold close in my heart: my late grandmother, my son, my partner, as well as the family, friends, teachers, clients, and guides, who supported me throughout this journey, created a safe space for me, and challenged me to bring forward the essence of "me" into the world.

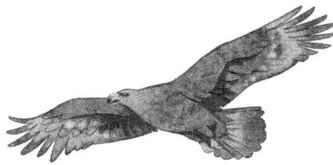

Contents

DISCLAIMER

This book is designed to provide information, motivation, and empowerment to readers. It is sold with the understanding that the author is not assured to deliver any kind of psychological advice (e.g., legal, medical, psychological) or be a substitute for professional assistance. No warranties or guarantees are expressed or implied by the writer in the content of this volume. The author shall not be liable for any physical, psychological, emotional, financial, or commercial damages, including, but not limited to, special, incidental, consequential, or other damages. The reader is responsible for their own choices, actions, and results. Situations, people, and contexts have been changed as appropriate to protect the privacy of others.

Introduction
My Soul-Searching Quest

I can vividly remember everything about that day. "Melissa," my first-grade teacher, Madame Soleil, said, "the class will be doing Christmas activities now, and you're not allowed to participate." Visibly annoyed, she took me by the arm, walked me toward the door, and peered out into the corridor. She then told me to sit on the floor outside the classroom and to not make any noise.

I learned later that my family had told the teacher to remove me from all religious activities in the classroom. I shouldn't have been surprised. I knew my family was religious in a "different" way, and that we didn't celebrate holidays like other people. I've chosen not to reveal the religion I was raised in, because I don't want to bring it any negative attention. Some people thrive in the community, and it's an important part of their lives. I think it is important to respect that, even though I felt it was not a good fit for me.

Looking back, this is probably my earliest memory of feeling like I just didn't belong. I knew my community's rules were strict and had to be followed. But school also had rules, and sometimes they didn't match up. Was I the problem?

I sat in the corridor, with nothing to occupy my time or mind, and no idea how long it would be until I was allowed in the classroom again. My eyes wandered to the coats hanging on hooks and boots lining the wall, where I spotted this really cool lunch box. It was the only one with metal clasps and a pretty picture on it. I can't remember the exact picture; I just remember being drawn to this spot of vibrancy in a sea of the mundane. I couldn't resist. I just had to try those metal clasps. I got up and unbuckled the hinges to see how they worked. Closing it quickly, the buckles went SNAP so loudly that I jumped, then froze.

Sure enough, Madame Soleil came out. "What did you do?" she asked sternly. "Nothing," I stammered. She took me by the arm and brought me to the other classroom. Knocking on the door, she said, "Melissa isn't allowed to participate in Christmas activities, so I'm leaving her with you."

"That won't work," The other teacher replied. "I'm also doing Christmas activities."

Exasperated, Madame Soleil said, "Well I don't know what to do, so you take her."

The other teacher gave me a paper and pencils to draw with. I was mortified. I would have preferred to cut out and color Christmas trees with the other kids and not attract all this unwanted attention.

Through this experience, and many others like it, my family kept assuring me that being different would make me strong, but as a young child, I didn't feel strong. I felt ashamed. I was uncomfortable with myself both at home and at school.

Like most kids, I just wanted to fit in and feel like I belonged. I always felt like I was being watched and judged; that I had to do what my parents said and follow the religion if I wanted to "be a good girl." But at school, I felt like following my religion made me difficult to handle.

I don't think I ever had the clear thought of wanting to "just be me" as a kid, but I knew that I wanted something different for myself. I was tired of always having to do things that didn't feel right to me and of missing out on things I really didn't want to miss out on. I was tired of trying to be good and always feeling bad. I didn't know if I was the one that was wrong or if everyone else was. At one point—I'm not sure exactly when—I made a promise to myself that I would make it right. That I would make ME right. Or make my life right. Or be even better for others. Or something. Anything. Just to feel like I was OK.

At that young age, I knew I had to find my own way, but I didn't have any of the tools or guidance to understand what that really meant. In trying to become Me, I ended up looking outside myself and creating mask after mask of who I thought I should be. I wore those masks like armor, until they became suffocating.

Today, I know the value of honoring what makes us different; that our uniqueness is our greatest strength and acceptance has to come from within. I know that each one of us is enough, exactly as we are, and that we are worthy of belonging and safety, in all areas of our lives. I know that when systems don't work, we need to remake those systems, not try to reshape ourselves to fit them.

My struggle may be connected to growing up in a religious community that didn't feel right to me, but I know that this experience is not unique to any one community. It's a struggle that transcends religion, culture, nationality, gender identity, and so many other factors.

Throughout this book, I've capitalized "Me" and "You" to refer to that most authentic and joyful self that we are all meant to be, have the potential to be, and are worthy of becoming.

Though my journey began in first grade, it wasn't until much later in life that I started to feel like I could fully be Me, freely and unapologetically, not weighed down by others' expectations or my own limiting thoughts. In fact, it took a few rounds of burnout and hitting my own personal rock bottom for me to finally say, "Enough!"

Even then, after a lifetime of looking outside myself trying to find myself, where would I begin?

It turns out my starting point was the one place I was most afraid to go searching: within me. It all starts within. I know this because I've lived it, and along the way, I have become a guide for others and had the immense privilege of witnessing their journeys of self-discovery, of dropping those heavy and carefully constructed masks, and of bringing their beautiful, unique selves forward into the world.

I'm sharing my search for myself to hopefully inspire you to look behind your own masks to discover the incredible, brilliant, deeply human, and deeply worthy YOU waiting to step into the light.

One of the bravest acts of self-love a person can undertake is to decide to just be themselves. I know that's easier said than done. It takes the courage to be vulnerable, the willingness to explore, and the openness to accept what you find with love. All of that is within you, and when you connect within, you not only tap into your best self, but are able to inspire those around you to tap into their best selves as well.

Everyone's journey to themselves is different. This book won't tell you who you should be or exactly what your journey should look like.

Instead, I hope it will serve as guidance to reconnect with yourself and uncover the You within.

Congratulations on taking this step and enjoy the journey!

PART I

Why Can't I Just Be Me?

Mover and Shaker?

Seven years ago, I opened my laptop and started writing.

The words flowed from my fingertips like it was meant to be. It felt right. It felt like fate. I was doing exactly what I was meant to be doing.

And it ended in tears.

Let's back up a little, to a time when a voice inside me started whispering that I had a story to tell. The voice was telling me I needed to write about a painful, but transformative, chapter in my life. A time when I felt I had hit my lowest low. It was the story of how I found myself a single mother to a four-year-old boy, with two divorces behind me, stuck in an unfulfilling career.

It was also the story of how I pulled myself out, through taking brave leaps of faith and leaning into the most vulnerable parts of myself. That experience had been raw, filled with shame, and deeply rooted in painful childhood experiences. Yet, here was this voice, demanding I expose my vulnerability to the world.

Again and again, I pushed the voice aside. But it kept coming back. What started as a whisper became a roaring thunder. I wasn't crazy about writing a book. I had married young, divorced young, married again, divorced again, had a child, started a business, made mistakes, trusted the wrong people. All of those decisions were wrapped up in feelings of shame and unworthiness and limiting ideas about who I was supposed to be. It was that painful story that the voice wanted me to tell. The story felt too personal, with details I hadn't even shared with my closest friends. But the voice persisted.

Eventually, it drove me to that fateful day in front of my laptop. As I typed, the chapters flowed, and the voice calmed. I felt good. Cathartic.

The end result was my first book, I Attract What I Am: Transforming Failure Into An Orgasmically Joyful Life & Business, which launched in July of 2016.

It took a lot for me to write that book. I had to shut out the negative voices and potential naysayers to focus on the positive and get my story out there. I tried to surround myself with positive people. People who would encourage and support me. Still, I hesitated many times before finally publishing. I went from "yes" to "no" moment to moment. "Do it! You have a lot of people to guide and inspire!" the voice insisted. And so, I did.

On the afternoon of July 23, just a few hours after the Amazon launch, I got the news. My book had become an Amazon international bestseller and was a #1 HOT New Release and #1 Mover and Shaker! I couldn't believe it. All my hard work and attention to my inner guide had paid off. Or so I thought.

That very same day, I received harsh criticism from people I had never expected. People really close to me said I had shared too much; that my openness was disrespectful to some of my relationships.

The feedback was painful. I had tried so hard to be mindful of the words I used and the details I shared in order to respect the privacy of others. I had bottom-lined as much as possible, left out names, held back identifying information, and had been careful to only share what was directly relevant to my own experiences. I simply wanted to tell my story so that others could see that transformation is possible. I had lived it, and I wanted to share the steps I took so that others could transform their lives and create their own joy.

Why did this feedback hurt so much? I started to doubt everything: myself, my inner voice, my intentions, my coaching, my choices, my relationships, all of it.

At the time, I was in the early stages of my energy medicine exploration, and I sought the advice of a shaman I had been working with. I was shocked when she, too, said I had shared too much!

It was like salt in a wound. I valued her opinion, and her opinion was that I had been wrong to share my truth the way I had. She had been one of my rocks, and now I was swirling in self-doubt. My inner Saboteurs were having a field day. Had I made a huge mistake? Should I take the book off the shelves, or edit it and release an updated version? I felt like I was in a dark pit with no idea how to get out.

A few weeks later, the shaman came back to me. It turned out she had had a concussion at the time I had asked for her guidance, and after recovering and tuning into her higher self, she went back to my concerns and felt she had made a mistake. She said that, in her opinion, what I had shared was OK.

Had this happened a few years earlier, I would have buried my feelings and abandoned the path that had brought them up instead of reaching out for support. I would have retreated into my comfort zones and old patterns, telling myself that nothing good comes from rocking the boat. Even after all my hard work, I did cave to the pressure a bit. I made some small edits to the book and released an updated version. They were minor changes but changes I wouldn't have made if I hadn't let the criticism get to me. Back when I had first heard the call to write the book, I had ignored it over the thought of what people might say. Writing a book at all, and then keeping it on the shelves, albeit slightly self-censored, felt like progress.

This time, I had turned to the Universe and asked for guidance. What was happening? Why was it happening? What did I need to learn from this? Those were the questions I brought to my shaman and what kept me curious instead of closed off.

Although I was making progress, I certainly did not feel like the author of a hot new release. Instead, I felt like my whole existence was being questioned. What if the shaman had not come back to me with her concussion confession? Would I have let self-doubt take over? Would I have abandoned my journey? I had achieved something amazing. Something that felt right for me and had come from my truest and best self. Why couldn't I enjoy that? Why were other people's opinions affecting me so deeply? I had worked hard to strengthen myself, so why could other people still take power from me so easily?

The pain continued. And deepened.

After a few weeks of questioning, confusion, stress, crying, and generally feeling terrible, the Universe came to me with a strong voice: "You did the right thing. This was just a test to stay true to yourself, no matter what people around you say. Even those closest to you."

I breathed a sigh of relief. I knew that voice. I hadn't heard it in too long, but now it was strong and clear. However, it was the shaman changing her opinion—saying that what I had written was OK—that initiated this clarity. I couldn't help wondering why her initial opinion had affected me so deeply. Why was I giving my power away? Why hadn't I trusted my inner voice from the start?

And yet, that voice reminded me that, despite all the hurt, I was still standing. My "worst case scenario" had happened, and I was OK. Hurt, but OK. I still knew I had done the right thing. My inner voice had led me to a difficult place, but it was not wrong.

As a coach, I help people, every day, to tune out negativity and not let it affect them. I help them see that it can't be taken personally; that what people say is often a reflection of their own circumstances. How could I let a few naysayers get to me? The answer is, I'm human. No one is ever done growing and learning. We all have ups and downs. What's important is to create from the downs to grow into the ups.

Sometimes people look at coaches, healers, and therapists as gurus. As though we always have the answers, never faltering or experiencing self-doubt. And yet, we are human. We are living our lives, making mistakes, and generally being far from perfect.

With my first book, some of the feedback I got was that people could not believe some of the obvious mistakes I had made in my relationships. Others told me that I looked like I had it all together and figured out. What I can tell you is that I am no guru. I don't have all the answers, and, oh boy, do I make mistakes.

Although . . . are they really mistakes? If you learn from what you experience, isn't that growth? An opportunity to share what you've learned with others? That's what I mean by "creating from the downs." When you falter, find ways that it can bring clarity to your path or value to others. When things go well, ask yourself how you can create more of it. Grow into your ups!

There will always be someone to question your decisions. Recently, I decided to sell my house and move into a condo. I can't count the number of people who told me that was a ridiculous idea. "Why would you do that? Usually, people do it the other way around!"

I get it. It may seem more "normal" to increase, rather than decrease, your square footage. That just wasn't what felt right for me, though. This was what I'd found fit the lifestyle I envisioned for myself and my family. Maybe it looked absurd to someone else, but I'm not someone else.

There's a saying. It's one of the most powerful I have heard: You have to be at your strongest when you are feeling your weakest. I don't know its origins, but it has helped me get through my darkest moments. During those times, I kept my focus on what I wanted to create in my life and drew strength from that vision.

When I was six months pregnant with my son, an ultrasound revealed two potential red flags and a 90% chance that there was something wrong. My doctors strongly urged me to have an amniocentesis, which increases the risk of miscarriage. It had taken me two years to get pregnant, and I wanted my baby so badly. But forgoing the amnio might mean a delay in treatment if there was something wrong.

I did the test. And it was hard. Not the test itself, but waiting three weeks for the results was agony. Especially as there was a risk that I could miscarry at any point.

I was definitely feeling at my weakest but also feeling like I needed to be at my strongest. If I did miscarry, I wanted my baby to have had the most peaceful in-utero life possible. That meant drawing on my full strength to make myself as peaceful as possible. I looked for joy wherever I could find it, telling myself that if I felt it, he would feel it too, and that was what was most important.

Through the sadness, the fear, the uncertainty about the future, I kept leaning into my strengths to move forward.

Dr. Dain Heer, an internationally renowned author, speaker, and facilitator of consciousness and change, teaches us to keep asking questions such as, "How can it get even better than this?" (Heer 2009). I love the phrasing of this question. It empowers me to focus on all that I am grateful for in the moment, and all the possibilities ahead. It's a question that reminds me of my power to continually take authorship of my life; to make things happen for me instead of to me; to put myself in the CEO seat of my own life. It's a powerful question because, no matter where I am, it helps me see where I need to go. It helps me catch glimpses of even the faintest light in the darkest room, so I can start pushing myself toward it.

Every time the negative voices crept back in, I would ask that question: "How can it get better than this?" The answer was not in those voices. The answer was in my big picture vision—the end result I wanted to create. I kept visualizing that result and focusing on where I wanted to go. And it helped. It helped pull me away from negativity and back onto my path.

CEO of Your Life Coaching Tip:

No matter how hard things get, don't let negativity hold you back. Continually ask yourself questions that enable new possibilities in every situation.

Time to Take a Stand

Long before I wrote my first book, when I was still a kid, I was sure all I needed to do was turn eighteen and things would get better. I had always been the black sheep, the "problem child." I was often told that my behavior was impacting my siblings and my family. If I questioned authority, I wasn't "setting a good example." If I misbehaved, I was "making the family look bad." I was told I didn't know how to listen; but what was I supposed to listen to, when so often the answer I received was, "Because I said so?"

On the other hand, I was consistently doing well in school, so how "bad" could I be?

In my mind, I just needed to turn eighteen. If I were an adult, my decisions and opinions would be respected, wouldn't they? But while getting older altered my circumstances, it didn't change anything inside me. Looking back, I can clearly see how much I expected external circumstances to heal me. But the truth is, we can't wait for the next birthday, year, fiscal quarter, paycheck, or relationship. We must drive our own change. If we don't heal at our core, we will continue to respond to our circumstances, whatever they may be, from that place of hurt. Either your heart can guide you or your hurt can guide you. I was letting my hurt guide me.

Accept What Is to Change What Is

The leadership practice known as "bounded optimism" has shed light on why my youthful positivity continuously led me into deeper and deeper disappointment. The idea is that you must have hope about the future and accept the present circumstances—optimism bound in reality. Bounded optimism is also known as the Stockdale Paradox, after Admiral James Stockdale (Collins 2001). As a prisoner of war in Vietnam, Stockdale was faced with the challenge of communicating hope in circumstances that felt hopeless. He noticed that those who were unrealistically optimistic—believing they would be home by Christmas, for example—tended to fare worse than those who accepted reality. By balancing messages of hope with acceptance of the facts, Stockdale was able to truly support the men imprisoned with him and lead them through the crisis.

The fact is, we can't change what we won't accept. To create real change, we must figure out how to work from where we are. Bounded optimism is fully, even brutally, honest about the present while staying hopeful about the future.

We hear a lot these days about "toxic positivity." I believe bounded optimism is the answer. Toxic positivity requires ignoring reality, pretending everything is fine. It shoves aside the most empowering aspect of any struggle: the journey to overcome it. Phrases like "good vibes only" send the message that difficult thoughts and feelings are unwelcome.

With bounded optimism, it's OK not to be OK. To feel anxious. To grieve what you had, or what you had hoped for. To make mistakes or be uncertain about what to do next. Just remember that whatever comes, you get to decide how you will respond. You can't change what you won't accept. Accept what is and accept that you determine what you do with it.

Believing that turning eighteen would change my life dramatically overlooked the truth that I was still stuck trying to do the "right" thing. When it came to choosing a field of study after high school, I couldn't even pick the "right" program. I was still expected to be someone I had no desire to be, still trying to fulfill those expectations and wondering why I still felt so unhappy!

Growing up, I used to collect postcards of all the cities I wanted to visit. I dreamed of becoming a flight attendant, having adventures, flying in and out of exotic countries, and exploring unique cultures.

I also loved helping people. In high school, I was selected to be a "go to" student that others could turn to when they did not feel comfortable sharing things with the school counselor. I even received training so I would be equipped to handle issues that came my way. I understood the responsibility of helping others through fragile situations, and I loved being there to support the people around me. My humanities teacher, Judith Castle, was the first person in my life to suggest I study psychology. It was the first time I'd even considered it, and it excited me right away. Ms. Castle was one of my favorite teachers. I loved her classes and felt that she was someone who was truly in my corner.

It was no surprise, then, that when choosing a field of study, I was torn between psychology and tourism. (Back then, "Tourism" was the name of a college program here in Canada. It has since been renamed to "Hotel Management and Tourism.") It was also no surprise that the adults in my life—my teachers, religious leaders, and most of all, my parents—had their own opinions, advice, and expectations, which they expected me to listen to.

When I suggested studying psychology, family members told me my budding interest was merely an expression of my maternal instincts, and that most people who study psychology don't make a great living. When I brought up tourism, they asked me, "Why limit yourself? Do your Bachelor of Commerce. It will open so many more doors for you. Business knowledge is the basis of everything, in every industry. Once you complete that degree, then you can choose to go into tourism or anything you want."

These weren't just suggestions. My parents were funding my studies, and they did not want to pay for a program they didn't feel was best for my future. When I made plans to get a job and pay for my studies myself, they weren't happy; they told me they would prefer I focus on my studies exclusively.

An agreement was finally reached, with a caveat. I had to write and sign a "letter of release," saying that I knew what I was choosing to study and would not come back later in life to blame them for not pushing me to make a better educational choice.

Writing the letter brought out so much self-doubt. Were they right? Working while studying, though doable, would be a struggle. Wouldn't it be smarter to get a more general business education? Was I being naive? Would it be a huge mistake to follow my interests instead of my parents' "safe" advice? Was my inner voice—the inner excitement guiding me—the voice I should be burying?

Ultimately, I determined that, although it didn't feel right in my heart, it was good advice. I followed my family's guidance, although I did apply my own twist by choosing a program called Fashion Marketing. The program had a strong business element, but also many opportunities for creativity.

After that, I got a Bachelor of Commerce degree. The Bachelor of Commerce degree made me miserable. I was still far from what I loved, and the courses in finance, statistics, and operations felt like drudgery. Looking back, the business knowledge I gained has come in handy, especially as I started my own business. However, could I have come to this same point (or an even better one) by a path of my own choosing? A path that was enjoyable and energizing? That avoided years of struggling against my true self to fit someone else's beliefs and values?

We are where we are because of everything that has led us to this point. My education has, undoubtedly, given me much of the stability and flexibility I needed to create the career I am enjoying today. But that doesn't change the fact that I spent years ignoring my own passions; interests I could have pursued from the beginning. And while I don't dwell, I do call on those memories at times to remind myself of how draining it felt to follow someone else's path instead of my own. Why did I keep ignoring my heart and allowing other people's voices to be more powerful than my own?

My career took me from entry level positions all the way up to vice president: in start-ups, where I could wear many hats, and Fortune 500s where I had more specific roles. I worked in management, leadership development, HR, and business development and operations, in industries ranging from cosmetics to travel to technology. I enjoyed each of those roles, at least for a time. I learned a lot and gave a lot. But as time went by, I began to see that success doesn't just come from titles or salaries, especially if the soul is craving something different.

I am grateful to my family for their financial support. I know many people don't have the same advantage: a university education resulting in a career path that was stable and financially rewarding. It allowed me many freedoms and opportunities that should be universal but just aren't. Financial support is a significant advantage, which I've benefitted from at some points in my journey. However, I've lived without it many times. What I've learned is that, as beneficial as financial support is, it is equally true that financial securities alone won't make for a satisfying and meaningful life.

Today, in my coaching practice, I see this again and again: clients in Fortune 100 companies, with lucrative jobs, at the top of their fields, who are just exhausted and burnt out. Almost always, a huge part of the equation is that they pursued financial stability to the exclusion of all other considerations. They either didn't think much about their lives outside of work or assumed that everything else would fall into place once the money question was solved.

But it didn't for them, just like it didn't for me all those years ago.

As my career grew, my mental, emotional, and spiritual energy steadily dried up. A good education followed by a good career was supposed to equal a good life, but nothing felt right. I knew something had to change.

Then life really happened. And fast. In just one year, I was divorced (for the second time), a single mother with primary custody of a four-year-old, and in a toxic work situation that required a job change ASAP. If ever there was a time that I needed to get real with myself, this was it.

I had done everything "right": I had pursued the more traditionally respected educational path. I had accepted lucrative positions at well-known companies. I had married, become a mother, bought a house. I had taken the traditional path that so many parents want for their adult children. And what my parents wanted for me came from a place of love. Having struggled in their own lives, having seen their parents struggle, they wanted an easier life for their own children. I am grateful for that love, and I do not discount the role their persistence and hard work played in the successes I have enjoyed.

The challenge is that their vision of what a good life should look like didn't work for me. When I found myself living inside of that vision, I discovered I didn't feel good in that life. Behind closed doors, that "good life" didn't look so great either. The tension between their vision and my lived experience made me doubt myself, and I spent a lot of energy beating myself up for somehow getting it "wrong."

My partner at the time, let's call him "John," and I had many differences. After our son was born, those differences became even more pronounced. Our parenting approaches were not aligned, and we argued often. We never really worked anything out. When John got upset, he just wouldn't talk to me for about a week. He would avoid me like the plague. I had to pretend whatever we argued about didn't happen. It was the only way we could go back to our daily routine. Everything was shoved under the carpet. I didn't feel safe to be myself or to speak my truth. Our son was up at least five times a night during the first year; I had gone back to work when he was five months old and was so drained I could barely get through the day. I needed support, and I felt John just didn't seem to understand. Looking back, I probably stayed in the marriage about three years longer than I should have. I was afraid to face my family as a "failure," which was how I was thinking of myself.

Even after those three years, it was John who ultimately left. At the time, I was working for a small company and had become good friends with my boss. Our relationship was strictly platonic, but John found it uncomfortable. It's possible he had been looking for a way out and decided to take the opportunity. I can't say for sure.

My boss's relationship was also struggling. I'll call him "Mark" and his partner "Julie." Julie was uncomfortable with our relationship as well and gave Mark an ultimatum: either I had to go, or she would. Mark and I talked it over, as friends, and it felt clear that we had zero romantic interest in one another. Still, we could understand, on some level, why our partners felt uneasy. John and I weren't right for each other and didn't have a strong marriage to begin with. On Mark's side, Julie might have just been uncomfortable with the level of emotional intimacy working closely with a colleague can create. I can't tell her story; all I can say is that, ultimately, Mark and I decided that I would look for another job, with his full help and support.

I was lucky; I know there are people out there who've had similar work experiences and not been treated fairly. Mark helped me find a good job that would not be a step back in my career in any way and continued to check in with me and be a source of support afterward. We even still work together from time to time today.

But even with that support, it was still a major upheaval. During the divorce, my ex did not fight for custody. I asked for primary custody, and John just went along with it. In order to keep some stability for my son, I also bought out John's share of the house. I don't regret it and am grateful I had that option, but it did create a significant financial strain. And, just when I needed a sense of stability more than ever, I was facing a massive shift in my career. I felt like every rug beneath me was being yanked out at the same time.

Having spent so many years living for others and disconnected from my true self, I was on the verge of burnout even before that storm hit. I was exhausted, drained by trying to hold everything together—until I couldn't anymore. I felt like I had fallen into a pit. In the community I was raised in, divorce is only an option in cases of physical abuse or infidelity. In any other circumstance, divorce meant failure. And this was my second divorce. I imagined people looking at me thinking, "How much more of a failure can you be?"

On top of that, I was alone as a parent for the first time. Without a partner, there was no one else to share childcare and housework. While I managed to keep going through the motions, I felt like I was doing it with a ten-ton weight on my shoulders. I didn't know how to ask for help, and I am grateful, every day, for the friends who stepped in with support without waiting for an invitation. At one point, I did reach out to a healer, Marie Danielle Boyer, and she all but carried my heart through this period. I distinctly recall one morning when I felt like I couldn't even get out of bed. Life just felt like too much. I called Marie, and she performed a healing over the phone, which gave me the strength I needed to get up and keep going.

On the outside, things probably didn't look too bad. The house was clean, my son was cared for, the bills were paid. Inside, I felt beyond overwhelmed. I felt like I was in continuous fight-or-flight mode.

Part of me wanted to wallow in that pit, but I had a son to care for and a life I still desperately wanted to live. Despite fear, fatigue, and self-doubt, I got up. I kept myself busy, running from my thoughts, doing what I needed to do to keep all the balls in the air, and in the process, remaining numb to the reality of it all. Instead of wallowing, I shoved myself into a hamster wheel.

There's a thing that happens when you close yourself off from feeling the bad things: You end up closing yourself off from feeling anything, good or bad. That's where I was. The pain of feeling like a failure, the shame of never being good enough, the weight of responsibility . . . it had become too much. I made myself numb just to keep moving.

I wanted to encourage my son to follow his passions and not perpetuate a cycle of playing it safe and sidelining dreams. It was not enough to want that life for my son. I had to show him. It was time for me to take a stand. I started with clarifying my stance on how I would parent and then worked on how I would start to finally just become Me.

The people around me were clear in their opinion that my youth and inexperience made me incapable of making good decisions. I didn't share those beliefs and knew I wasn't going to raise my son by making all the decisions for him. I also knew I wouldn't make him bend to my will. I strongly believed that my role as parent was guide, not dictator. I wanted my son to learn tools in childhood that would serve him into adulthood, empowering him to be responsible for himself and feel ownership of his choices. And if I wanted that for him, I would have to learn it for myself too.

I also know that I don't have to be perfect for him. It's good for him to see me struggle, make mistakes, and try again. It's good for him to see that the universe doesn't collapse when we don't get it "right" and that we can be flexible and adaptive—at any age—in finding our way.

Secure in my parenting philosophy, I looked at what I could do to model it for him and started with examining what I do for a living.

My first step was finding a new job. I was lucky enough to choose from two job offers: one with the start-up, the other with a more traditional and secure insurance company. The insurance company promised the kind of safety I had been raised to value; but the start-up offered flexibility around start and end times, which was vital to me as a single parent. I took the start-up job.

I knew working in a start-up carried some risks, but the founder had offered me a signing bonus and guaranteed that I would be paid regularly. Sure enough, paychecks started becoming . . . not regular. Financial stability had been drilled into me as one of the most important things to strive for in life. I had always been careful about savings, and a regular paycheck wasn't just a measure of success. It was a measure of safety.

The lack of stability was jarring. It wasn't just me this time. I also had my son to care for, and I was solely responsible for his safety. But I was also responsible for being at my best with him. I wanted to be present and happy for him. I wanted him to have a parent with the energy to be with him, the patience to guide him, and the joy to show him how wonderful life can be. I knew that if I dove back into the corporate world, I wouldn't have much of that to give him.

I stuck with the start-up and the unstable paycheck. I compensated by dipping into my line of credit and starting my own coaching business on the side. I knew I wouldn't be able to build up any savings, and that I'd be going into debt, at least temporarily, but I also felt that I couldn't go back to the same path of burnout and unhappiness. I had to find another way to create safety for myself and my son AND create a life I enjoyed.

Again, I recognize the advantage of having a line of credit to fall back on and the opportunity to start creating a business while working. I had a credit line as a safety net, even if it didn't always feel like one. For some people, my decision may not even seem like that big of a risk at all; for others, it's unthinkable. What I know is that, for me, it meant turning my back on everything I'd been told was safe, smart, right, wise, and logical. It was so scary. But turning back to "safety" felt even more terrifying.

Working at the start-up also gave me another advantage: it allowed me to learn all aspects of running a business. Seeing entrepreneurship in action inspired and taught me and was instrumental in bringing me to where I am today.

I won't dig into the ins and outs of starting and growing a business, but just know that I am not suggesting it was a simple mindset shift. It was a lot of work and facing my fears.

And before I even started, I had to become a coach.

You know the expression, "You have to walk before you can run"? Well, when I said it was time for me to take a stand, that's really what it was. Making the choice to start pursuing what I wanted truly felt like standing on my own for the first time.

Now I had to learn to walk.

When I decided to enroll in the Coaches Training Institute, I once again got an earful of advice. My father said, "Why would you spend so much money to become a coach? Coaching is just a fluffy thing. It's a fad. Do your MBA. That's something credible and solid."

Again, I knew the advice was meant well. Although not having his support did hurt, this time, after some reflection, I recognized it as his point of view, based on his experiences, and it did come from a place of love. To him success and stability came from working in a bank, and that's what he wanted for me. It was not what was best for me. Just imagining going back to business school put my stomach in knots. To my father's credit, I should note that his opinion of coaching has evolved, having seen the industry grow over the years. At the time, the industry was not given as much credit as it is today. Now, he has even suggested teaching my son about coaching skills!

Although I hadn't yet learned it as a leadership practice, I was starting to shift my mindset into bounded optimism. I was learning to accept my circumstances for what they were without losing sight of the possibilities for creating a future even better than I imagined.

I could see the path that was right for me, but could I take it? Was I brave enough to take that first step? To start walking? How could I believe in myself if the people who raised me—who had known me longer than anyone— didn't believe in me? (Or so I felt.)

CEO of Your Life Coaching Tip:

Where do you need to take a stand in your life? Listen to that voice inside you. What step can you take—however small—that is led by your heart, not other people's opinions?

Parent, Raise Thyself

I will never forget the day. March 17, 2011. I had just finalized my second divorce and become the primary caregiver to my four-year-old son.

I found myself sitting on the hardwood floor of the house I now owned—along with the bank—by myself, with my head in my hands, asking, "How did I end up here?"

Everyone has different perspectives on divorce and single parenthood. The end of an unhappy marriage is a complicated thing. For me, the message I was raised with was that marriage, family, and a good job were the only things that mattered. It didn't matter if it was a happy marriage, a peaceful family, or a job that didn't suck the life out of me—in fact, none of that was even mentioned. It was just "marriage, family, job." If I had failed at that, I had failed at life.

I felt ashamed. I can't put into words how low I felt; how hard it was to put one foot in front of the other. It felt like my body was made of lead, every movement taking more energy than I thought I had.

From where I am today, I can see that I really did have things working for me, even if I didn't see them at the time. I had asked for primary custody and got it, without a fight. I had my house. Yes, it had dragged me further into debt, but keeping it had been a viable option for me. I had friends and colleagues who wanted good things for me. I had my health. I had my mind and my heart. I had possibilities.

One of the things I started doing at this time was working with a life coach, which a former colleague had suggested to me. I had never heard of life coaching; it was a revelation to me that there were people who had made it their mission to guide others. I found the idea comforting. If this was an entire industry, surely I couldn't be the only person struggling to hold my life together!

Coaching was a huge step for me. It was so different from anything I'd done before. I remember my first coach, Meisha Rouser, giving me assignments that felt completely alien. Visualize "future me"? Imagine I had a magic wand and anything was possible? Make decisions from some imagined future instead of my current reality? *What*?

I kept going back to that saying: "Insanity is doing the same thing over and over again and expecting different results." If everything I'd ever been taught about success wasn't working for me, what did I have to lose by doing things differently?

My coach asked me a lot of questions that, frankly, scared me at the time. She would have me visualize this ideal, completely unrestricted life for myself, and then ask me what was holding me back from creating that.

What I eventually came to understand was that my own beliefs were sabotaging me. Also, those beliefs weren't really mine. They'd been given to me, and I had never thought to question them. I didn't have to hold onto what I'd been raised with. I didn't have to believe that divorce was a failure. If I wanted to, I could start believing that I was at the beginning of a journey, instead of at the end of one. I could raise my son the way I wanted to, even if it was different from how I was raised. I could decide on my own beliefs and my own way of being and parenting.

To be clear, my parents were loving in their own way. They were, I believe, driven by fear. Fear of the consequences of straying from tradition. That came across to me as disapproval; a sense that I was not good enough as I was. Their love language was praise for being "a good girl." When I misbehaved or questioned adult authority, that praise was taken away. In those moments, it felt to me like love was taken away. As an adult, when I tried to follow the path they had set out for me, I'd failed. It felt like love and acceptance were being ripped away, and that left a big wound.

I understand today that many parents are driven by fear and tradition. How my parents parented is probably how they were parented, and so on. How we parent—and do most things—reflects where we are on our journey. That's where our intention comes from. Being different was, to my parents, as dangerous as running into traffic. Their intention was to protect me from that danger; it came from love as much as it came from fear. But what makes us different is nothing to be feared. It's how we bring the greatest value to our lives and those around us. That wasn't something my parents could see from where they were. In my parenting, I want my son to know the value of his uniqueness. To embrace everything about himself. I was determined to be the link that broke that cycle. To not raise my son from my hurt or my fear, but from my heart.

Whenever possible, I try to provide opportunities for my son to try things and see how they fit. I want him to build the inner strength and confidence to venture out into the world, centered and solid. I tell him to stand up to anyone—even adults or authority figures—if something doesn't feel right to him. I tell him to do what feels right for him and to let me know if ever I ask him to do something that makes him uncomfortable. I encourage him to tune into his inner voice and to connect with it. I respect his boundaries and when he speaks, I listen so that he knows that he is seen, heard, and accepted exactly as he is.

5 Cornerstones for Parenting

Coaching is what started to give me a framework for how I wanted to parent. It helped me start to articulate my own beliefs and values, build them into a foundation, and bring them forward with confidence. I didn't have a lot of confidence in my parenting at first, which fed my self-doubt. I spent a lot of precious energy worrying about my decisions. Coaching empowered me to divert that energy into being even more present for my son, and for myself.

One of the lessons I applied to parenting was what's called Co-Active Leadership. Co-Active Leadership operates on four cornerstones (Co-Active Training Institute n.d):

1. Treat everyone as naturally creative, resourceful, and whole.
We are all doing our best from where we are. Sometimes, we need guidance or support in reconnecting with our creativity, resourcefulness, and wholeness.

2. Dance in the moment.
This is about flexibility and agility in the present moment with what comes up. We can learn from the past and plan for the future, but it's in the present that life really happens.

3. Include the whole person.
All parts of us are worthy, acceptable, and deserve to take up space.

4. Evoke transformation.
Every challenge is an opportunity to grow, and good leaders work with us to move in that direction at difficult times.

In my own coaching practice, I include a fifth cornerstone:

5. Partner with your body.

The sensations we feel in our bodies in reaction to different situations is our intuition speaking to us. By partnering with our bodies, we can make sense of that intuition and make decisions with greater clarity.

Learning these cornerstones and how they applied to leadership, I couldn't stop thinking about how I wanted to raise my son. Although I had many ideas for how I wanted to do things differently, I now had a framework to follow.

I began to think of the cornerstones in terms of parenting:

Cornerstone 1 - Children are naturally creative, resourceful, and whole.

I've always believed that I have more to learn from my son than he does from me, and I strive to treat him like a speaker of truth. Really young children don't have all the mind clutter that adults and older children have. They experience their inner world more clearly. If they say they're happy, it's because they're happy, not because they think that's what's expected.

My son is now a teenager—and still awes me with his wisdom—but even when he was very small, I would listen in wonder as he spoke without filters or inhibitions. He would say what he was thinking and express his emotions as they came up. I aimed to always accept what he had to say as his truth and let him take the lead in solving his problems.

When he would tell me he felt scared, instead of saying, "There's nothing to be afraid of," I'd ask him what he was afraid of, where he felt the fear in his body, and what might help him feel safe.

If his drawings weren't working out, I would ask him what he wanted to do next. Sometimes he'd want to start over, sometimes he'd want to keep going, and other times he'd want to stop all together. And so, he would.

We started doing fire ceremonies— a mindfulness ritual where you symbolically "burn" difficult emotions—when he was just five years old. He really enjoyed this, and when something would happen that stirred up big feelings, he would come to me and say, "Mom, can we burn it?"

I won't say I got this perfectly every time, or that he always had answers. I will say that when I treated him as naturally creative, resourceful, and whole, he would bring those traits forward, like they were just there, waiting to be tapped into.

Cornerstone 2 - Dance in the moment.

Life is unpredictable. Life with children is even more so. When I reflected on how my parents raised me, I realized they spent a lot of time in the future. They had many concerns about the kind of adult I would be. I understand these concerns, especially now as a parent. However, I also feel that life is more joyful if childhood is as much a focus as eventual adulthood.

One day, when my son was napping, I decided to nap too. When I woke up, I found that he had not only woken up before me, he had also figured out how to climb out of his crib, AND had found the paints, AND had begun finger painting on the wall.

I could just imagine some parents in that situation. I am sure many would take it in stride. And I am sure others would feel anger over the mess or worry that a child painting on walls clearly didn't have enough discipline and fret about what kind of person that child would grow up to be.

I have to say, my first reaction was to freak out a bit on the inside.

But then, I brought myself into the moment and reminded myself that I was looking at a toddler, not a future adult. He didn't know not to paint on walls. It was my job to guide him, and this was a teaching moment. I could teach him the very practical lesson to not paint on walls, and the lesson that love persists even when we make mistakes. I told him his painting was beautiful, and then directed him to a large paper so that we could continue painting together. I eventually cleaned up the mess, but also kept a small portion of his finger painting on the wall. It's his art, and I love to look at it.

To give my son love in that moment was like a hug to my child self. Raising my son differently was more than just a parenting philosophy. It was helping me heal.

Cornerstone 3 - Include the whole person.

I strove to follow his interests and strengths as much as possible. Initially, I put him in soccer and hockey because that's what other parents were doing. But he wasn't really into it. He preferred karate, so we hung up the cleats and skates, and picked up a *gi*. And by age ten, he'd earned his black belt. Later, in high school, he wanted to study video game programming, which was offered as a concentration option at his school. He thrived in his class.

I believe that when children do what they love, they're happier. They also get to experience enjoying work. Earning his black belt was hard. Learning to program video games was challenging and new. He did the work for both with joy and pride.

I was never taught that work was something I could choose based on what brought out my natural talents. I was taught to always prioritize security and stability. One of my parents had lived through the Hungarian Revolution; the other lived through a tumultuous time in Greece known as the Greek junta, or Regime of the Colonels. They knew what life was like when security and stability were scarce. They just wanted better for me. And that meant ignoring what I was drawn to, even though I ached for it.

I remember hearing Deepak Chopra once say that he told his children to do what they loved, and if they can't make a decent living, he would support them. By following what they loved, they ended up doing so well that they never needed his help.

I feel what's important is to support children emotionally and spiritually. If you can do so financially as well, that is a bonus. Speak to them with love and validate their wants. Embrace the wholeness of who they are, always.

Cornerstone 4 - Evoke transformation.

Life can be hard. School can be hard. Friendships and relationships can be hard. Each of us have ups and downs along the way. We can't shield our children from the downs. Difficult times can help us appreciate the good in life and give us the best opportunities to grow. Think about it: our most significant personal growth usually doesn't come from the easy times but from times of struggle.

The way I was raised, mistakes and disobedience were a big deal. Positive interactions were withheld if I misbehaved, and I would feel like my world had been turned upside down. It was an awful feeling that followed me into adulthood. I was always afraid to mess up or disappoint someone because what would happen next? You cannot learn from a mistake when you're busy beating yourself up about it.

When my son would make a "mistake," (I put this in quotations as I believe there are no mistakes, just opportunities to learn), my initial instinct was to get impatient. Instead, I would take a deep breath, remember the parent I wanted to be, and do my best to work from that place.

It didn't come naturally at first, but it always felt right to me in the aftermath. Guiding my son through calmly and lovingly assessing his "mistakes" gradually soothed my child self. Slowly, that instinctive fear began to soften, and I found myself speaking to myself the same way I spoke to my son. My own "mistakes" were OK too. I could clean up my messes, find lessons, and move myself forward. I must admit this has been an ongoing journey. I am not all the way there yet, and it will take time. But I make it a priority to work on it continuously.

Cornerstone 5 - Partner with your body.

Growing up, I wasn't specifically told to ignore the messages of my body—those intuitive feelings telling me if something was right or wrong. However, my family and community did give strong and repeated messages about the type of behavior that was expected of me. It was made very clear that this obedience, this "good behavior" was more important than anything else. I learned early to ignore my feelings and my intuition.

With my son, starting when he was very young, I tried asking him questions that would help him tune into his body. I would ask, "How do you feel about this? What is your heart telling you?" And then I would listen and acknowledge what he was feeling. He now has the experience to start with curiosity when feelings come up, and he leans into it.

Having this framework has been empowering for me. It isn't a step-by-step guide; children are their own, complex human beings. As parents, we must be open to who they are and who they are becoming. We have a job to protect them, guide them, and teach them about how to move through the world. And, I believe, we have a responsibility to help them do that without losing pieces of themselves.

I am not a parenting expert in any way, but as a former child, I can tell you that being heard and loved matters to children. As a parent, you need to parent in a way that feels right for you and your child. Think back to how you were raised. What felt right to you that you can carry forward? What felt wrong to you that you can learn from and do differently?

There's a poem by Khalil Gibran called "On Children." I love every word of this poem, but there's a particular passage that has stuck with me:

"You may strive to be like them, but seek not to make them like you.

For life goes not backward nor tarries with yesterday.

You are the bows from which your children as living arrows are sent forth."

Children growing up is life going forward. My son is not me. He is a completely different person, and that's such a wonderful thing. My role isn't to mold him; it's to help him grow fully into himself, exactly as he is meant to be.

Here's a short exercise for you. Write out your parenting beliefs. If you've never really thought about them before, try giving yourself an easy number to work with. Ask yourself, "What are my top three parenting beliefs?" Then explore how they are working for your family, and if there is something you would like to change:

My top 3 parenting beliefs are...	How are they currently serving me and my family?	Do I want to bring this belief forward into the future?

If YES, how can I bring it forward even more?	If NO, what belief can I replace it with, and what will it look like in practice?

If You Are Not Currently Parenting

Our experience of being parented is foundational. It informs—in one way or another—the rest of our lives.

If you aren't currently raising children, I encourage you to do the above exercise and put yourself in your parents' or primary caregivers' shoes. What would you say their top parenting beliefs were? How did those beliefs serve you? If you were to take over from your parents, would you bring those beliefs forward? If not, what beliefs would have served you better?

Doing this exercise can help you start to heal wounds you've carried forward. Even with the most wonderful parents anyone could hope for, we can end up carrying things into adulthood that just aren't right for us. Maybe it's something huge, like your worthiness to receive love, or maybe it's something small. Maybe your parents always said owning a pet would be too much work, and you've carried that forward without realizing that you can make that choice for yourself now. Whatever it is, it's OK to stop carrying it.

The people who raise us are our earliest experience with authority. With leadership, really. Whether we're conscious of it or not, our minds will relate future experiences with authority to that earliest experience. What worked for us in childhood can evolve with us as we become adults. We might feel instinctively distrustful of authority figures or yearn for their approval. We might become people pleasers or struggle to hold boundaries. Whatever it is, healing it matters.

It's OK to need to parent ourselves a little—or a lot—in adulthood. It doesn't even mean your parents were wrong. It could just mean that the world is different today and your child self needs permission to adapt to it. The difference is, you're the only one who can give yourself permission now.

> **CEO of Your Life Coaching Tip:**
> You don't have to keep carrying beliefs that someone else handed you. Keep asking yourself, "Is this belief truly mine? Is it serving me? Do I want to keep carrying it, or can I shed it?"

When Opportunity Knocks, Will You Answer?

The thing about turning points in life is that you either don't expect them at all or you don't expect them to "turn you" in exactly the way that they do. Over the years I've hit many of these points—points where the Universe knocked me over the head with something—and one thing they all have in common is that they hold vast amounts of potential. But they only have power if we're ready and willing to seize what they're trying to show us.

I was at leadership training with the Co-Active Training Institute in North Carolina when I got a call from my mom to say that my grandmother was not well. She had pneumonia, wasn't talking, the antibiotics weren't working, and her kidneys were failing. It was a Thursday, and my flight home was booked for the following Monday night. I told her I would go see my grandmother as soon as I arrived.

"She probably won't make it till Monday," she said.

My body froze, and I felt a pain in my heart.

Although my grandmother was ninety-one years old, I could not accept her dying without one final goodbye. Throughout my life, she had been my rock; my safe space. She always gave me unconditional love, accepting me fully for exactly who I was, even when I messed up. She stood by me no matter what, encouraged whatever choices I made, and gave great advice, all while respecting who I was and the path I was on. She was always joyful, positive, and important in my life, especially growing up. She was full of life and shockingly funny. "You need to eat well," she told me once. "You burn one thousand calories when you have sex." She was full of surprises!

What was I to do?

I was part of a ten-month leadership program in a tribe of twenty-six people that I loved. Missing a training day would mean I wouldn't be able to continue with the same tribe. The program was truly meaningful to me; going in, I had felt in my heart that this would be one of those big turning points in my life. I felt like I truly needed to be in that space with those people. They were quickly becoming something more than just a cohort. We shared vulnerabilities, supported each other, and let ourselves be supported. These were (and still are) powerful, meaningful relationships.

At the same time, I couldn't imagine not saying goodbye to my grandmother. Finally, I decided I had to ask for help from the Universe and the people around me. Like many people, asking for help is outside my comfort zone, but I knew I couldn't do this alone.

In leadership training, we were taught that asking for help is important, because no one can become a great leader by doing things alone. To continuously move forward, learn, grow, and succeed, we must lean into the experience, strength, and energy of the amazing people surrounding us.

I asked my tribe mates if, at the end of our training day, we could gather to put out good thoughts for my grandmother. They all happily agreed. We sat in a circle. I had a picture of my grandmother and lit some candles. I shared stories about her and how she inspired me. She had grown up in Hungary, and told me stories about working in a hospital during the Hungarian Revolution. Bombing raids would interrupt her shifts; she would duck and cover, praying hard for her own survival. She was lucky; so many around her weren't. She never forgot how grateful she was to be alive in those moments. Her unending positivity was so inspiring. She was a role model of strength, love, joy, and lightness. Always her truest self, bravely and unapologetically. Turning toward gratitude no matter what.

One of our teachers (in leadership we call them "Leader in Front") presented the idea that, if it felt right, I could open it up so we could send love and positive vibes to other people who were sick or had passed. Quite a few tribe members talked about friends or family that were not well and needed love sent their way. We sent lots of love to each of these people. It was a beautiful evening, and we all connected on a deeper level.

Continuous Miracles

I made it home, and my grandmother was still alive. Not only was she alive, but her fever broke, the antibiotics kicked in, the light had come back on inside her, and she started talking again!

I knew that things could have turned out differently and that I would have felt devastated to lose my grandmother without a final goodbye. However, I also felt the support I'd received from my tribe mates fostered a sense of connection with a powerful network. I knew that if my grandmother had passed over, my tribe would continue to be there. To me, it felt like the Universe was showing me how to thrive through life's challenges, not just survive. Connection was the answer.

Over the following days, I heard from members of my tribe that they had also had profound experiences within their relationships. Sharing their love and fear for people close to them seemed to heighten their connections and bring richness to their lives.

Then my Leaders in Front told me:

"What a wonderful example of the impact of intention."

"Wow, you are one powerful leader. One of your quests is to bring more of this into the world."

More of this?

The intention circle I had initiated is a practice of energy medicine. I believe in the metaphysical element of these practices, but these practices have value whether or not you believe in their metaphysical aspects. The sharing circle was about supporting each other through difficulties and a hallmark of many energy healing practices is having a compassionate guide to help you through challenging emotions and experiences.

That said, lots of people call this type of thing "woo-woo" and don't take it seriously. You especially don't see it often in corporate settings. "Energy medicine" is the term I prefer, and it's an important part of who I am. But I still thought . . . bring more of this into the world? Although I believe in my practice, I wasn't sure if it was something I was ready to bring forward. I was worried about labels, about judgments and assumptions. How could I bring this into corporate environments?

I know the business world well, having spent more than two decades deep within it. Did I really have it in me to not only bring those two parts of myself together but to also bring them out for the world to see?

What I do know is that the effects of the intention circle for my grandmother were exponential. Members of my tribe were inspired to start putting their true selves out there. I had brought forward a part of me that I had felt I needed to hide. That action enriched my relationships within the group and seemed to spark a mindset shift for others. The power of many people sending love and light into the world can create real shifts! When you drop your masks; when you do things from the heart that you truly believe in; when your thoughts, words, actions, and soul are aligned; everything is possible.

I believe my grandmother came to this earth for many reasons, one of which was to look out for me. She supported me unconditionally for all the years we had together. Even as she seemed ready to leave this world, she gave me a wonderful gift: a situation where I had to ask for help, create true community, and be entirely Me.

Bringing the Essence of You Forward

Since this experience, I've decided that one of my leadership quests is to bring more of this part of me into the world. At the time, I wasn't fully clear on what this would look like, but I promised myself to bring a little more of it forward each day by sharing my true beliefs—no matter the situation, supporting others that share their true selves, and inspiring others to bring their true selves forward. Just as that powerful experience presented itself to me, I was also opening myself to more opportunities that may come my way.

I had felt that a turning point was coming for me, and it did. I had felt that my tribe was meant to be a powerful part of my journey, and they were. But not in a way I had ever imagined. The Universe is funny that way. Even when it fulfills our expectations, it does so in ways we never expect, which is why it matters that we're ready for those turning points when they come.

So, *when* do you dare to bring the true You out? The end goal is "always," but that starts with small, courageous steps that get bigger and more frequent as you go along.

Are you ready to be daring? To bring more of the essence of YOU forward in your life, relationships, home, work, and community? To seize what the Universe has to give you? To lean into opportunity, not knowing what the outcome might be?

CEO of Your Life Coaching Tip:

Opportunity will always come knocking. It's up to you to decide if You answer, or if you let your fear, hurt, and limiting beliefs answer. When you make the choice to drop your mask and open that door as your truest, most vulnerable self, you begin to create true, heartfelt connection that empowers genuine shifts in your life and the lives of those around you.

Self-Acceptance and Self-Authority

"A leader is someone who takes responsibility for their world."

—The Co-Active Leadership Handbook

One of the first things I learned in leadership training was this definition of a leader: one that puts the primary focus on leadership of the self. It's a concept I lean into in all aspects of life. All positive change starts with knowing and accepting ourselves fully, then bringing that forward with confidence. It is our knowledge of self that empowers us to be intentional in how we show up and in the impact we have. This also means taking full responsibility for our world. It's the starting point for everything. Once we do that, if we choose, we can then have a greater impact when leading others.

What it Means to Take Responsibility

Many people feel challenged by the concept of responsibility because there are so many things in life that we simply do not control. We don't control other people's behaviors or attitudes. We don't control the weather or traffic. We don't control people getting sick, neighbors being difficult, the way we were raised, and so on. All of that is valid, but it misses the one thing we do control, no matter what is happening around us: how we show up. That's what it means to take responsibility for your world. It's to recognize that how you show up, respond, behave . . . it is all within your control, and *taking* full control is how you have the greatest impact on your own experience of life.

Taking responsibility isn't about taking on blame or having to fix everything (oh boy, has that been an empowering lesson for me!). Rather, it's being in the moment, accepting that everything around you *is* happening, and making conscious choices about how you show up and respond.

Stepping Into Yourself

Do you ever have days where you have an idea of what you want to get done, but then a thousand little things get thrown your way that have you feeling endlessly busy, without accomplishing anything meaningful? Or you are so overwhelmed and paralyzed by those thousand little things that you aren't accomplishing anything meaningful, and now you also have a backlog to deal with?

That's how your days unfold when you are not authoring your life. Instead, you're allowing everything and everyone around you to write your story. Once you embrace responsibility for your world, the next step is self-acceptance and self-authority.

Self-acceptance means fully accepting all parts of you: your light, your dark, the good, the bad, the ugly, the messy, the klutzy, the weird, the wonderful. Self-authority is self-acceptance in action. It means actively and intentionally bringing all parts of you forward. This demands a shift from living from the "outside in" to the "inside out."

Many of us live from the outside in without even noticing it. Something happens and you react. You drop what you're doing, switch focus, adjust your approach. While you do need to deal with what is happening in the moment, living from the inside out requires taking a critical moment before you act to check in with yourself. If you don't take a critical moment to look inside, you can end up making decisions that move you further away from what you truly want.

Stories of Disempowerment

To "disempower" means to take away someone's authority or agency to act, making them less likely to succeed. If we look around the world, there are endless examples of disempowerment. Many of us, when we see these situations, are able to say, "That isn't right. That needs to stop." But are you able to recognize when you are the one being disempowered? What about when the person causing you to be less powerful is *you*? We have a word for this—self-sabotage—but it sounds aggressive. We tend to think we would never sabotage *ourselves*. But when we replace "self-sabotage" with "disempowerment"— taking away our own authority—and reflect on the ways we speak to ourselves and how that translates to our choices and behaviors, it becomes clear how we can slide into disempowerment without realizing it.

Put the power where it truly is: within you. If you can disempower yourself, you can empower yourself.

So why is it such a struggle? It comes down to patterns. Patterns we grew up with, patterns that surround us, patterns we fell into during difficult times. When we experience patterns repeatedly, they can become the lens through which we see the world. We believe that this is just the way things are. That's what keeps us stuck—the belief that there is nothing we can change about our world. The truth is, you create your world. Whether you empower yourself to make things happen *for* you or you disempower yourself with a mindset that things just happen *to* you, you are creating your world.

Stepping into self-acceptance means accepting what happened in the past. There's no changing it now. There's nothing you can do about the things you cannot control. But you are always responsible for how you show up, and you always have been. Once you accept these two truths, you can step into self-authority and start consciously choosing how you show up in order to create your world intentionally.

The Triangle of Disempowerment

Although you may not have heard the phrase, the "triangle of disempowerment" is a pattern you're probably familiar with. If you're not currently stuck in it, odds are you've been caught up in it before. The concept was first described by the psychiatrist Dr. Stephen B. Karpman, who referred to it as the "Drama Triangle" (1968). The Drama Triangle framework has been used to understand a number of different relationship dynamics. I prefer the term "triangle of disempowerment" because it tells you, right away, why you don't want to let yourself get caught in this type of dynamic. It may sound harmless to enjoy a little drama from time to time, but when you realize the ways it can take your power away, you're better positioned to take back authorship of your life. The triangle is a story with three main characters:

1. The Victim

The Victim has a mindset of "I'm not good enough and I never will be. The cards are stacked against me, there's nothing I can do about it, and I can't do what others can do." The Victim absolves themselves of responsibility for their world and believes others must help them because they are unable to help themselves. They may also use blame, claiming their eternal victimhood is caused by forces beyond their control.

2. The Rescuer

The Rescuer derives self-worth from what they can do for others and doesn't see themselves as having value outside that. Often, the Rescuer mindset is a way to avoid responsibility for personal growth by claiming responsibility for the growth or success of others. The Rescuer needs to be needed, sometimes adopting the role of martyr, claiming they need to sacrifice themselves for the good of others.

3. The Perpetrator

The Perpetrator believes the world is dangerous and everyone is out to get them. Perpetrators are often aggressive and combative, believing they need to strike first so no one can take advantage of them. The Perpetrator puts others on the defensive, thereby creating a world for themselves that matches their belief. The Perpetrator's greatest fear is losing control and becoming a Victim.

These three characters need each other to complete the story. The damsel in distress is victimized by the villain and must be rescued by the prince. It's a story we're so familiar with that we don't realize how destructive it is in the real world. (In life, of course, the damsels, princes, and villains can be of any gender identity.)

We can become stuck in this triangle, caught in patterns or stories that play out again and again. Think about the Bermuda Triangle, where even expert navigators can be caught in the chaos, unable to find their way out. There are many ways we can get stuck in life; different patterns or beliefs that leave us feeling like we can't move forward. The triangle is not the only way to get stuck, but it is an incredibly common one.

Here's what it can look like to be stuck in the triangle: The Victim tells themselves they are incapable of overcoming challenges. But life is full of challenges! With that "I can't" mindset, the Victim goes out into the world encountering challenge after challenge, "proving" their story to be true. Anyone who helps the Victim proves they cannot help themselves. Anyone who doesn't help proves that the world is stacked against them. They are stuck.

Many Rescuers are in close relationships with Victims—a friend, family member, partner, adult child, etc. The Victim's continual needs and "inability" to care for themselves reinforces the Rescuer's story that they are needed and that they cannot prioritize their own needs or wants because the Victim comes first. They are stuck.

The Perpetrator enters every interaction ready for a fight. When confronted with this aggressive approach, people either fight back or flee, proving to the Perpetrator that this is the way of the world. They are stuck.

Here's a key truth: What you put out into the world reinforces the story you tell yourself. There's incredible power in that. When you recognize the story you're stuck in, you can recognize and accept the ways you have created it. If you created that for yourself, you can create anything for yourself.

Whether you are stuck in the triangle or stuck in some other way, navigating out is all about awareness of the patterns holding you in disempowerment, so you can start making empowered choices. *Worthy* choices. That is what self-acceptance and self-authority look like in action.

Worthiness and Getting Unstuck

Getting unstuck happens when you take full responsibility for your world. Not *the* world, but *your* world. Your mindset, attitude, beliefs, inner leadership, choices, the way you show up . . . all of that is your world, and it is all within your control. Seizing that is how you break patterns of disempowerment.

Let's go back to the Bermuda Triangle. Lacking clarity and awareness, our disempowered pilot is just going in circles. Once our pilot escapes the triangle, however, everything shifts. Outside the triangle, there are still challenges to overcome, but the pilot can see the way around or through them. Empowered by clarity, they can make choices with their destination in mind. Getting out of the triangle means recognizing the patterns you are stuck in, your responsibility for them, and that you are worthy of moving forward.

What the Victim, Rescuer, and Perpetrator have in common is that all three look outside themselves for their sense of self-worth. But worthiness comes from within. It's rooted in honoring your true self, humanity, unique strengths, passions, and life purpose and choosing to be the author of your own story.

Putting your self-worth outside yourself is a disempowering choice. It puts the control in someone else's hands. The way other people show up, their behavior, their choices, all speak to your worth as a person when you are in the triangle. Just as you put it in their hands, you can take it back. That choice is yours and always has been.

Non-Engagement

Looking back from where I am now, I can see many times throughout my life when I was caught in the triangle of disempowerment, including one particular experience with a client.

As a coach, it is part of my purpose and passion to be in service to others. It is an honor to serve as a guide and to learn alongside them. However, one lesson I've really had to learn is how to hold healthy boundaries. Sometimes a client will have expectations that go beyond the bounds of the coaching relationship, wanting me to be available to them twenty-four seven.

I remember one particularly challenging Friday evening. A client was going through a hard time. She spent much of our session crying, and my heart went out to her. When our time was up, I felt like I couldn't just let her go. I ended up staying with her for two and a half hours. It wasn't just the extra (unpaid) time; because the call ended so late, I was exhausted when my son woke early the next morning. The same client asked me again to do an evening session, and again I agreed. And *again*, the time went over. I found myself exhausted in the morning, wondering why I'd accepted a meeting that I knew was going to leave me drained and frustrated, rather than energized and available for both my son and my other clients.

Coaching is something I do because I genuinely want to make a difference in people's lives. That passion isn't something I can just turn off when the timer is up. It wasn't just setting boundaries with my client but also setting (and holding) boundaries with myself on when I would work and for how long. I wanted to support my client but not at the cost of my own well-being. I had to remind myself that every time I said yes to her, I was saying no to something else.

But I didn't come to that realization right away. I had to reach out for guidance. It was my teacher, Karen Johnson from The Four Winds Society, who suggested I take a step back from the situation and practice non-engagement.

Non-engagement means not letting yourself be drawn into conflicts that lack any meaningful grounds. When you are set off or rubbed the wrong way by another person, rather than engaging with their behavior, explore how your discomfort may highlight a part of yourself that needs to grow or heal.

The triangle is an energy vortex. When you engage with it, it sucks in your energy—your power—and you can lose connection with your intuition. It's a reaction to trauma or toxic circumstances. It's how you survived once, but you no longer need that particular coping mechanism. Visualize the person you are caught in the triangle with and say, "I didn't deserve any of that. I am taking back my power."

You can say no. You can say HELL no. You can choose to let go and move out of the vortex under your own power. Say to yourself, "I am through playing these roles. I am done." Visualize pushing the energy sucking triangle away, further and further, until it disappears.

When you stop spinning in that vortex with people, they will look for another partner. When that happens, choose to act as an observer. "There they go, caught up in the triangle." Observe without judgement or engagement. See it for what it is, and simply state your observations, like an objective scientist: "I see how you are trying to make me feel small." "I see how you are trying to make your problems mine." "I see how you are trying to make my pain your burden." "I see what this is, and I am not participating."

The other person's behavior isn't personal, so try to depersonalize it if it helps. Conjure up the narrator of a nature documentary, observing the various rituals and behaviors of their subjects as they watch from a safe distance. Have compassion in your observations but also courage in holding your boundaries.

With this mindset, I began retelling the story from an approach of non-engagement, and I realized that I had been playing both the Victim and the Rescuer in this relationship with my client. I realized an old pattern had re-emerged. A pattern of feeling responsible for someone else's experience. What was different this time was that I had cultivated the tools, self-awareness, and self-acceptance to be continually checking in with myself. Instead of unconsciously regressing into old comfort zones, I knew I had to consciously take authorship of my world; to tell the story in an empowering way.

In my new telling, I met an opportunity to continue to heal, and I embraced it. I met an opportunity to practice holding healthy boundaries; an opportunity to lead by example in holding those boundaries; an opportunity to meet someone with compassion and curiosity, while holding firm in myself, not giving pieces of me away; and I embraced these opportunities with joy.

By taking responsibility for my world, I also stepped more fully into my purpose of being in service to others. This client's expectations of me were coming from an unhealed place, and I could best be of service by guiding them to heal themselves, to take back their own power and step into self-acceptance, self-authority, and self-worth.

Many years ago, if I had been faced with similar circumstances, I would have stayed quiet, wanting to keep the peace and to keep others happy, and then silently dwelled on the relationship in my mind. In the past, I would have prioritized being *seen* as worthy over actually *feeling* worthy. This time, I made the choice to break old patterns.

At the end of the day, we are the stories we tell ourselves. Change your story, and your journey changes.

Now, when I find myself sliding into old patterns, I use a three-step practice to shift myself forward. This practice was inspired by the book *Co-Active Leadership: Five Ways to Lead* (Kimsey-House 2011).

Step One: Take full responsibility for your world.

In the story above, I started out flip-flopping between feeling taken advantage of and feeling responsible for someone else's experience. Yes, there were factors outside my control, but I could control how I chose to show up in that discomfort.

Step Two: Embrace full self-acceptance.

A key factor of self-acceptance is honoring your feelings. I accepted the feelings that came up for me as neither good nor bad and instead as simply things that needed my attention. I accepted that my body would constrict and react strongly whenever the relationship with my client came up. These feelings were my inner leader speaking to me, and it was a voice I needed to hear.

Step Three: Put it into action through self-authority.

Self-authority is self-acceptance in action. I could bring self-acceptance forward by setting clear boundaries with myself and my client and trusting the process.

Stepping Into Self Worth

When faced with a situation where you might normally adopt one of the triangle roles, take a mindful moment and ask yourself, "Do I want to be SEEN as worthy, or do I want to BE worthy?" No one can give you your worth. No one can fill that void for you, just as no one can take your worth away. You are worthy, just as you are.

You are worthy of working on yourself.

You are worthy of taking action.

You are worthy of change.

You are worthy of help, support, and guidance in healing yourself, and you must take full responsibility for making it happen for you. The way out of the triangle is to lean into yourself. And you are worthy of that too. Commit to changing the story you tell yourself. Do so with intention and repetition, embedding a new story of empowerment that will see you bringing more of your true self forward, building healthy relationships with yourself and others, and creating a world for yourself that is fulfilling and joyful.

Imagine you are born with two books. In the first book is everything you cannot and will not control. It tells the story of where and when you are born, the family you're born into, your genetic makeup, the things that will happen around you, and so on. There is nothing in this story that you control; it will simply play out as you go through life.

The second book is the Hero's Story. This book is blank, because it's yours to write. As you go through life, it fills up with everything you *can* control. It tells the story of what you do with everything in the first book—how you respond, the choices you make, the relationships you cultivate, the way you show up, the values you embody. You are authoring this book every day of your life, whether you do so consciously or not. Most importantly, you can change the course of the story at any moment.

If, up until now, you've been telling yourself a story of disempowerment, start telling a new one. In your new story, make yourself the Hero. Unlike any of the players in the triangle, the Hero depends only on themselves for purpose, choosing to take their story where they want it to go.

Here are four steps you can take right now to start telling a new story:

Step One: Identify a limiting story you tell yourself.

Step Two: Write a new story that empowers you.

Step Three: Find or create affirmations that reinforce your story of empowerment. Write out your new affirmations every day for four weeks and put them somewhere you can see. This ensures that they sink in.

Step Four: Set aside a single minute each day to take some deep breaths, speak your affirmations to yourself, and to lean into that energy as if it's already in your life.

Going forward, as that first book unfolds, continually focus on ways to make your story—that second book—one of empowerment. How do you become your own hero?

CEO of Your Life Coaching Tip:

You are already authoring your own story, and the only thing holding you back from writing yourself as the hero is you. Commit to taking full responsibility for YOUR world, starting now.

PART II

Nine Core Lessons

Tune Into the Leader Within

The empowering thing about authoring your life is that you already have a leader within to guide you: the voice inside that knows, intuitively, what is right for You. It is your inner GPS, just waiting for you to tune in. Transforming your life is not about creating a different You. It's about connecting with the authentic You that already exists, then leading yourself from that place.

In the next chapters, we will walk through nine powerful lessons that will help you better understand which elements of your life today are authentically You and which are not. I will guide you through reconnecting your mind-body-spirit-energy wholeness, strengthening the inner connections that empower a life of authenticity, and begin bringing your truest and best self forward to transform your life in a way that works for You.

Where is Your Leader Within?

All of us are born with an inner leader that we're meant to grow with. So, what happened to it? Where did it go?

Many cultures take an approach to child development that splits the self. When we act impulsively as children, we're punished or shamed. The resulting suppression of our impulses is called "impulse control." This term, however, is inaccurate: suppressing something is not taking control of it. A child acting impulsively is reacting to messages within themselves—messages from their leader within. Suppressing those messages leads us to look externally for acceptance and validation instead of developing skills like self-confidence and self-leadership. We learn to constantly ask ourselves whether we're fitting in. If we do stand out, it must be in an accepted and externally valued way—good grades, athletic ability, musical talent, or other skills that our peers will accept and admire. In adult life, that translates to seeking validation through job titles, salary, house size, high end purchases, social media presence, or other appearance-based factors.

On the other hand, some cultures take an approach of guiding children to accept and interpret the messages within them. When a child acts impulsively, the child is encouraged—without shame—to explore the thoughts and feelings that led to the behavior, so they can notice it and make better choices in the future. To put it simply, they learn to address, not suppress; to tune into the messages of their inner leader.

There was a beautiful piece written in *Today's Parent* magazine by Andrea Landry, an Indigenous mother from Poundmaker Cree Nation, located in Saskatchewan. She wrote that in Indigenous kinship practices, "Kids are raised to express all emotions, freely and openly, and parents teach them healthy methods to express those emotions" (2021).

Then there's the Bubup Wilam Aboriginal Child and Family Center in Australia, which focuses on supporting children and families through traditional practices and values. *Supporting Vulnerable Babies and Young Children: Interventions for Working with Trauma, Mental Health, Illness and Other Complex Challenges* includes a case study of the center which explains that, "The children are learning that emotions are not bad things and that it is OK not to be happy sometimes, as well as learning that there are different ways to deal with disappointment. When a child becomes overwhelmed and can no longer self-regulate their emotions, educators step in and support the child to take deep breaths, offer physical comfort by rubbing their arms or legs (or cuddling younger children), and speak softly to let them know they are safe, and that we will remain with them until they feel calm. If they are physically lashing out, we carry them safely to our Zen room, where adults remain with the child and talk them through the self-regulation process. Once calm, we talk to the child and together develop strategies for the future and remind them of these strategies in their everyday play" (Music and True 2019).

In your own parenting—or even with yourself—you can start to integrate similar practices with one simple, but powerful, change: naming emotions without judgment. That might sound like, "It looks like you're feeling frustrated. Let's take some slow breaths together, then you can talk, and I'll listen." It seems simple, but it's a huge shift from just trying to get kids to calm down, and it starts building a foundation for healthy emotional regulation.

This teaches true self-control: when you can notice what's coming up, tune into the messages, and consciously choose how to respond to them. When we act impulsively, that is reacting, not responding. When we shove impulses down, that too is reacting, not responding. When you connect with your inner leader, you recognize the divine wisdom within your amazing self. The people, relationships, and communities around you still matter, but they do not hold the key to your self-worth.

Identifying Your Leader Within

Have you ever ignored a gut feeling? Or felt compelled in a certain direction but talked yourself out of it? I have. Many times. When it came to relationships, jobs, finances, pastimes, pretty much everything. I shoved my inner voice aside and looked for external guidance instead.

Those feelings inside you are your leader within.

Stop. Shutting. It. Out.

Stop shoving it into the background. Bring it forward and pay attention. Trust what it's telling you. Your leader within is your inner guidance and is foundational to all the lessons going forward. It will help you make clear, confident decisions rooted in self-awareness.

For me, ignoring my inner leader kept me stuck in a life that was disconnected from myself. I wasn't happy. In fact, I was dragging myself further and further from happiness. Making the choice to really tune into (and follow!) my own leadership was a massive shift, but I was desperate and determined. I was sure that if I kept listening to everyone else, I'd keep dying a little bit each day. For years, I had sensed my heart trying to get my attention, and I wanted to tap into what it had to tell me.

This new direction, this idea that I could be the one to call the shots, was foreign and scary. Sometimes I would sweep it under my mental rug. But, through much trial, error, and discomfort, I learned that when I finally started connecting with that voice, my entire life changed.

I realized something that I would lean on many times throughout my journey: if you want to succeed at something, you need to be OK with failing at it too. Whenever you try something new, you will make mistakes. No one turns their life around overnight. They try, fail, backslide, try again, and so on. Failure and success are not opposites;

failures are the stepping stones of success. It's in the getting back up, again and again, that we build resilience and new ways of being.

Connecting with your inner leader is a new pattern you're forging. You will make mistakes. You will slide back into old patterns from time to time. You will misinterpret some messages or let external factors cloud your vision. Accept failure as part of your journey forward. Keep tuning back in and trying again. In meditation practices, there's a common refrain: if your mind wanders, simply notice it and begin again. There is no real failure. Only being. If you wander from your leader within, simply notice it and begin again.

Practical Tools for Connecting with Your Leader Within

Replacing an old habit with a new one requires intention. Over time, the new habit will begin to feel reflexive. In the meantime, it's completely normal for the new habit to feel unnatural. That unnatural sensation can make it difficult to know if your new habit isn't right for you or simply isn't familiar yet.

There are four tools that will help you ingrain the new habit of connecting with your leader within *and* help you get clarity on whether something is truly right for you.

Tool #1: Mindfulness

A lot of people believe that mindfulness is time-consuming, like waking up at four in the morning to meditate. The reality is, mindfulness is simply about noticing things in the moment, and that can be as simple as a five second practice of stillness. Just five seconds, spent intentionally, can be enough for you to connect with the intuitive wisdom of your heart.

Whether you have five seconds, five minutes, or even a full hour, here are four ways you can work mindfulness into your daily routine:

1. Take slow, long, deep breaths. Often, we're rushed and take short breaths without even realizing it. Intentional deep breaths can be done anytime, anywhere, and have such a transformative effect. As you take your deep breaths, focus on your heart, focus on your stomach. It's amazing how fast you can get out of your head and reset.

2. Go out and experience nature. Nature is grounding. It connects us to the earth. Go outside, even if it's cold. Set the intention to pay

attention to each of your five senses. What do you hear, smell, see, feel, taste? Notice which way the breeze is going. Touch a tree. Sit or lie down. This takes you out of your thoughts and reminds you that you are part of something bigger.

3. Count to five. Five seconds is a lot longer than you think when you are experiencing them mindfully. The act of counting itself is a way to stay focused and present. Take the time to count out five full seconds. Those seconds are more powerful than most people realize.

4. Use mindful affirmations. You can create a whole new reality just by changing small daily habits. Mindful affirmations are one of those changes. Choose an affirmation that aligns with the experience you want to move toward. "I am enough." "My feelings are important." "I am loved." Affirmations train your brain how to think. The same way our childhood brains were wired through repetition, we can make conscious choices about how to *re*wire our own brains through repetitive, mindful, empowering affirmations.

Tool #2: Meditation

Meditation is a mindfulness practice, but it's a powerful one that deserves to be a tool all on its own. You may have heard of the concept of the "right" and "left" brain. In general, the left side tends to be more involved with reason and logic, whereas the right side tends to be more involved with creativity and intuition. In some early studies of brain activity, it was found that people who engaged in regular meditation had higher levels of activity in the right side of their brain than non-meditators had (Pagano and Frumkin 1977). We spend so much of our lives—especially our school years—focusing heavily on those "left brain" skills. Meditation helps us tap into that "right side" to start bringing all parts of our brilliance forward. Studies that use neuroimaging to examine brainwave activity have found that during meditation, our minds "step away from problem solving" (The Norwegian University of Science and Technology 2010). When we're in problem-solving mode, we tend to rely heavily on our left-brain skills, but by "stepping away" from that, we can tap into right-brain skills, which also have a lot to offer.

It's an active practice of intentionally carving out new neural pathways, like ski tracks in fresh snow. At first, the trail can be hard to find. But, as you travel the path over and over again, it becomes smooth and intuitive.

While I prefer meditating in the mornings to fuel me for the day ahead, meditation can be done at any time that works best for you. When I meditate, I feel I am charging my best self and getting into a mindset to respond, rather than react, to whatever comes up during the day. I don't talk to anyone or do anything in the morning before listening to a guided meditation. They are like soul food. By practicing meditation at times of peace, you open new pathways that prepare you to lead in times of stress, chaos, or uncertainty.

Here are just some of the benefits of meditating:

- Gain new perspectives on stressful situations.
- Develop ingrained skills to manage stress in moments of tension, pressure, anxiety, etc.
- Increase your self-awareness for greater self-acceptance and response-ability.
- Focus on the present to reduce mind clutter.
- Reduce the intensity and impact of negative emotions.
- Strengthen your imagination and creativity.
- Increase your patience and tolerance levels.

When author and activist Marianne Williamson came to speak in Montreal in 2022, she ended her speech with this powerful message: "Meditate in the morning and kick ass in the afternoon!" (An Evening with Marianne Williamson 2022).

If you have trouble quieting your overactive mind (I know I do), guided meditations can help remove all the clutter preventing you from connecting with your leader within.

My favorite meditation app is Insight Timer. It has a meditation for everything: recovery and healing, sleep, happiness, spirituality, stress and anxiety, creativity and performance, relationships, kids and teens, abundance, fertility . . . you name it, they have it.

It also helps to start small. If you feel you can't sit still for more than five minutes, then just do five minutes. Or three. Or two. There are many meditation apps, podcasts, and other resources available. If the first one you try doesn't feel right, try another. Like anything, it needs to feel right *for you.*

Most importantly, remember that meditation is not about clearing your thoughts, but about noticing them without judgement. It's our habit of judging thoughts and feelings the moment they come up that leads us to react instead of respond. By noticing without judgement, you empower yourself to start sliding into response-ability more naturally.

Tool #3: The Light Method

The Light Method is a technique I learned through Access Consciousness. Access Consciousness is an organization that provides different services and trainings in the realms of alternative medicine and personal growth. I will note that there is some controversy around the organization: its founder, Gary M. Douglas, has ties to the Church of Scientology. I am not endorsing Douglas or Access Consciousness necessarily; with any path I explore, I usually find aspects that resonate with me, and others that don't. The Light Method is a useful tool, and one that has served me.

When you need to make a decision or find yourself questioning a belief, quiet your mind and take a moment to see how the different answers, ideas, or scenarios feel in your body. Do they feel light? Do they feel refreshing or exciting? Do they give you a sense of calm, clarity, or joy? Or do they feel heavy? Does your heart rate quicken? Does your body start to feel unwell or weighed down? Does your inner vision feel cloudy or dark?

In both scenarios, your leader within is speaking to you. Lean into what it has to say. This is You speaking to You, and who has your best interests at heart more than You?

Think of something you've been struggling with, where there are different routes you can take. Close your eyes. Relax. Start with route number one. What does it look like? What could happen? Notice what your body is telling you when you tune into this option. Is it light? Exciting? Expansive? Or do you notice a tightness? Maybe your stomach clenching or your throat tightening? Then imagine route number two. What does that feel like?

The lightest path is the one you need to explore further. Especially during challenging times, when you may have to make decisions you have never made before, the Light Method is a helpful tool for connecting with your inner guide.

One way we can explain this light feeling is through research that suggests the brain is not the sole source of our inner experience and knowledge. We have neurons all throughout our bodies that sense, feel, remember, and send messages. Canadian Professor of Physiology and Biophysics, Dr. Andrew Armour, describes the neurons in the heart as fundamentally similar to the neurons in the brain. Based on his research, he coined the phrase "heart brain" (Alshami 2019).

We often treat intuition and logic as separate things. But logic *builds on* intuition. Intuition is what anchors logic to the here and now. We all know we shouldn't act on intuition alone, but we don't consider that logic alone isn't sufficient either. Logic on its own misses that fundamental connection with our world, our innate perception of what's going on around us. Intuition isn't *illogical*. It's *pre*-logical. It's the thing we're meant to tap into first, before we move into logic. That's what the Light Method helps you connect with; that part of yourself that is grounded in the moment and aware of what you need in your present to build your best future.

So, maybe when you are feeling light, that's the messages from all those neurons throughout your body finally getting through, telling your logical, overthinking brain what is truly right for you. When you experience that light feeling, listen to it. Hold onto it as you move forward. Know that this is the direction you are meant to go.

Tool #4: Name It to Tame It

Thoughts and feelings create your world. Those thoughts and feelings are fueled by observation, noticing not only what's happening around you but also what's happening within you. One thing to start noticing is all the thoughts that have been shaping your world, unchecked and unrecognized. The catch is, you must learn to notice them without judgement. Guilt, anger, shame, fear, sadness, helplessness . . . these feelings come from judgement and will only hold you back if you feed into them.

With "name it to tame it," you notice a thought, then name what your mind is engaging in. For example:

"Oh, I'm imagining."

"I'm telling myself a story."

"Oh, I'm judging."

"Hm, I'm assuming."

Say it to yourself in a light inner voice; simply observe the activity of your mind. Naming something really can stop it in its tracks or at least take away its power. Just as Rumpelstiltskin loses his hold over the maiden when his name is spoken, your subconscious thoughts lose their hold over you when you name them. In this way, you keep your mental chatter in check in a way that is kind to yourself, creating more space for nourishing thoughts to thrive.

This tool can be especially helpful in stopping resurfacing wounds from discouraging you. The deepest wounds take the longest to heal, and it's only natural that changing circumstances can expose them in new ways. You may want to have a phrase to repeat to yourself when you notice a wound resurfacing. Something factual and non-judgmental. "Ah, that's hurt coming up." Let the wound surface with love and acceptance so that it can be soothed, healed, and become a source of growth. By calming your mind in this way, you clear the air for your inner leader to shine through. Those thoughts just want to be noticed. Once you give them that, they can move along like clouds in the sky, leaving a vast horizon of possibility for you to see.

CEO of Your Life Coaching Tip:

Your leader within is You. Tune into it. Trust in your inner GPS. This is the path to truly honoring and being You.

Tune Into Your Shadow

The facets of ourselves lost in childhood can go beyond our inner leadership. What is shoved aside can encompass large parts of our humanity.

Many of us in coaching and healing refer to this realm of shoved-aside-things as the shadow. Pushing aspects of ourselves into the shadow leaves those connections starved for light and nourishment. By tuning into your shadow, you bring light back to those connections, allowing their true forms to regrow and bloom.

Accepting Your Shadow

Robert Johnson's 2009 book, *Owning Your Own Shadow*, has been a huge inspiration for me. It's where I first learned the true power of tuning into your shadow and accepting everything you find there as a critical aspect of radical self-acceptance. But what really is your shadow and what does it mean to accept it?

The shadow is everything we try to push aside; everything we believe needs to be denied or suppressed. The origins of our shadow are almost always in childhood. It starts with the things we're told are not OK. This can come from family, guardians, caregivers, friends, community or religious leaders, teachers, and anyone else of influence around you—usually adults, but also older children, siblings, or influential peers. This experience is different for everyone, although some things are almost universal. For example, many of us are taught that feelings like anger and jealousy are always inappropriate and that we shouldn't feel them at all, or that the demands of authority figures should come before our own feelings. Ultimately, we learn that to fit in and be accepted, we have to minimize these parts of ourselves, behaving as if they do not exist.

Here's the problem with suppressing or denying our shadows: our shadows are part of our whole selves. Your shadow and your light are not independent elements. A full day is not just daylight but also dawn, dusk, morning, afternoon, and night. A full life includes birth, death, and everything in between; a full human includes the shadow. Just as truly loving someone means loving all of them, loving yourself means loving *all* of yourself. Full, radical self-acceptance.

I use the word "radical" because it is so ingrained in our society to understand things in terms of good and bad that to accept *everything* as worthy truly is a radical stance. Your shadow is worthy because it's human; because it's YOU. Every single element of your shadow is worthy of your love, acknowledgement, and acceptance. It is worthy of your exploration. It is worthy of *being brought forward.*

Worthiness and What Truly Lives in the Shadow

When I bring up the idea of shadow worthiness, many people go straight to extremes. They will say things like, "But what if someone's a murderer or a thief? That can't be acceptable!" For most of us, what lives in our shadow is nowhere near those extremes, and yet we're so accustomed to hiding our shadow, and so afraid of owning it, that the very idea gets equated with things like murder in our brains.

Yes, there are some very, very wrong things in this world. I'm not speaking to those things. I'm speaking to the very human and very much worthy shadows within us. When you think about what resides in your shadow, what's so wrong with any of it? What really lives in that "unacceptable" place?

For many of us, what lives in our shadows are things like:

- Speaking up for ourselves.
- Prioritizing what matters to us over the comfort of others.
- Pursuing our passions instead of taking the safe route or following the "rules."
- Guiltlessly taking breaks instead of working into a burnout.
- Befriending people outside our circles.
- Noticing and exploring the full spectrum of our emotional experience, instead of suppressing negative feelings like anger or sadness.

What's so bad about any of that? There's nothing bad about having thoughts and feelings. I would even say that there's nothing bad about *thinking* about any of those really, really bad things. They're just thoughts, and everyone has them. It's what we do with our thoughts and feelings that can have a positive or negative impact outside of ourselves.

Yes, jealousy, judgement, resentment, anger, disappointment, and fear all live in our shadows, but the thoughts and feelings they bring are just messages. When we try to shove those things aside, our bodies try to get those messages to us in other ways. We can become passive-aggressive or defensive and engage in other self-limiting behaviors. When we simply accept the messages and hear what they have to say, we're able to choose how to respond with intention and clarity.

Accepting your shadow empowers you to understand the messages coming from those parts of yourself, giving you greater insight into your own inner experience; what matters to you, what you need to feel whole, and what's holding you back from bringing your best self forward.

Balancing Your Shadow and Your Light

Have you ever tried making big changes all at once only to quickly fall back into old patterns (or worse)?

This is because we aren't meant to live in extremes. Our bodies, minds, and souls crave balance. Whenever I've overworked myself, that period of overwork has always been followed by an illness, burnout, or extreme fatigue, as my spirit needs to balance out what I've pushed myself to do.

I must confess that I've done this repeatedly in my life. I keep saying that I won't let it happen again, but still, I fall back into the pattern. A few years ago, to prepare myself for a much-needed vacation with a friend, I worked double time, right up to the day we left. And I got so sick.

There I was, dipping my feet into the water of a beautiful North Carolina beach, but I couldn't fully enjoy it because my body was not cooperating. I didn't want to be that sick away from home, so my friend and I decided to drive for twenty hours straight to get back home.

And this wasn't the first time I'd worked myself sick. During my college years, I kept working and studying to get the high marks I was expected to get. I would get so weak from overwork that I couldn't even lift a glass of juice.

When my son was born, I went back to work after five months. I was still waking up with him during the night and pumping milk at the office. I was beyond exhausted, and this time, I had a fully dependent little person to care for!

What I've learned from that is that toggling between extremes takes a toll. We're meant to live in the middle of our unique extremes. That's not to say we're meant to compromise on things that matter to us. That's not what *your* middle is. Your middle is the place where you don't feel pulled to either of your extremes. It's the place where you feel at peace in your heart.

People who experience midlife crises often talk about doing the "right" things their whole lives and then just wanting to let loose or go crazy for once. This is a perfect example of trying to deny your shadow. When you spend your whole life suppressing natural parts of yourself, it's no wonder it eventually erupts in what looks like a crisis. It *is* a crisis! Accepting both your shadow and your light gives you clarity into what balance looks like for you.

You may be thinking, "I can't bring this part of myself out. It isn't OK. People will be upset, hurt, offended, or angry. They won't want to be anywhere near me." Or if you think, "But what I do *does* impact other people. I can't just go around doing and saying whatever I want, and I don't want other people doing that either!" I ask you to consider this: You already are pushing your shadow onto others. Whatever we suppress will find a way out. Always.

If you suppress anger at work, it could come out as road rage on your drive home. If you hold back disappointment in your relationship, it could come out as apathy at work. If you deny your passion in your career, it could come out as resentment toward those in your personal life. Or maybe it isn't spilling onto other people but into other areas of your own life. If you aren't pursuing your true interests, maybe that spills out as overspending on frivolous things. If you are suppressing wounds from your past, maybe that spills out as accepting less than you deserve in relationships.

I've often struggled to embrace my shadow in relationships with others. Growing up under intense pressure to meet expectations led me to become a people pleaser. That need to be what people expected me to be—and what I expected me to be—continued into my career. Usually at the expense of my wholly connected self.

I remember once rushing to meet up with a friend. I was exhausted and just wanted to go home to rest. But I had made a commitment, and following through on my promises is important to me. I showed up. And she forgot.

At first, I called her to see if she was OK. Something could have happened to her, after all. But no. She said she had been cutting the grass and getting things done around the house because her husband wasn't helping at all. She'd gotten tired and busy and just plain forgot our plan to meet.

This was far from the first time I'd heard this friend blaming her fatigue on her husband. Normally, I would have slid into coach-mode, setting my own hurt and frustrations aside. I would have asked powerful questions to guide her to find clarity, take authorship, and move forward. That day, however, I was so tired myself that coach-mode went right out the window. I blurted out, "I keep hearing this story over and over. When are you going to do something about it? If you stay with him, you will be tired for the rest of your life."

Oh my. She, understandably, did not take it well.

At first, I felt that I'd been unprofessional. But I needed to remember, in that moment, that I wasn't her coach. I was expecting myself to be Coach Melissa and only Coach Melissa, but I am also Friend Melissa, Parent Melissa, Melissa with Finite Energy Stores. Melissa Who'd Been Stood Up. I have many facets, and they deserve to come forward.

What I blurted out had come from my shadow self. It felt so freeing to let it exist, out in the open. Maybe I hadn't spoken in the most compassionate way, but I had spoken my truth and begun to establish an important boundary in that relationship. Yes, I could have spoken with kindness and still set a firm boundary. I could also have chosen to cancel when I felt too tired. Or I could have chosen to simply accept her reply and move on. Once I began to accept and embrace my whole self—shadow and all—these "shadow options" began to appear with greater ease and clarity in different situations. Mistakes I made as I moved forward could be learned from, but they were nothing to be ashamed of.

When you stop trying to suppress your shadow, when you own it and accept it with love, you get to decide how, when, and where it comes out in your life. This is how you take control of it and integrate it into your whole being. For example, if you often find yourself getting annoyed by other people, accept that as part of yourself and start exploring it. Ask yourself things like:

"What are my thoughts in those moments? What am I feeling in my body? What else is happening around me? What do I want to happen? How am I contributing to those moments, and how can I speak to myself with love while they are happening? What boundaries might I need to set with myself and those around me?"

Really get vulnerable with yourself and explore that shadow. Familiarize yourself with what's going on and find the good within it. Your shadow is filled with things that want to guide you in advocating for yourself, making decisions that align with your values and purpose, building healthier relationships, and so much more.

Shadow and Light at Odds

Sometimes, what lives in our shadow and what lives in our light can seem to contradict each other. A simplistic example would be your light wanting to be productive and your shadow wanting a Netflix binge. How do you accept that? It is important to remember one thing in these moments: accepting something doesn't mean you have to act on it.

Accepting everything within you means just that: accepting that it is there. Acceptance calms the inner battle. When you simply accept all sides—accept that there is duality within you—the sides stop fighting for your attention, and you're better able to find or create the space that is right for you.

You may love your spouse, for example, and be so grateful to have them in your life—*and* they may sometimes do or say things that are enraging to you. You might find yourself caught up in thoughts like, "How can I resent someone I love? I'm a terrible partner!" You may find yourself prone to mood swings, feeling extreme love in one moment then snapping at your partner in the next.

I know that sometimes when I look at my partner, I feel so proud of what we've created and grateful for the day he walked into my life. Then there are days when he doesn't pick up after himself—doesn't even notice he hasn't picked up after himself—and I just lose it. He knows I need a Zen-like space to feel at peace. Clutter is not Zen! And then, of course, I feel guilty. He really does try his best—he is just so busy, and the mess doesn't seem to impact his productivity. We just see things differently.

It's no easy task, but accepting that I can love someone AND feel frustrated by their habits AND still be committed to the relationship is freeing.

What if you just accept both sides? Accept that you sometimes feel angry or resentful and sometimes feel overwhelming love. Many of us are taught to restrain our emotions, meaning even strong feelings of love become suppressed. But these are fundamental parts of who we are. If you accept all parts of yourself, fully and without judgement— especially accept the parts that feel like contradictions—they will stop fighting with each other, and you can explore them more fully, to see what might be hiding within. Your two sides might also simply settle into new practices that allow them to exist together, peacefully. Just allow the paradox to exist. Stop fighting against what's naturally within you. Love and accept it instead.

Teaching Our Children to Love Their Shadow

If you are a parent, caregiver, teacher, or work with children in some way, you are in a powerful position to truly change the world. Imagine a world where people accept their shadows, learn from them, and respond to them with clarity and full self-awareness. A world of people who focus on showing up as their whole and best selves, instead of putting precious energy into upholding a certain persona. A world where people explore negative thoughts and feelings instead of letting them fester.

This world is possible, if we change the way we teach children about their shadows. The most important thing you can do is to be vocal in your acceptance of your own shadow, and in your acceptance of theirs. It's as simple as, "I'm feeling so angry right now. I need a minute to sit with this feeling and understand where to go next." Or, "You seem sad right now. I'll sit with you while you're having this feeling and you can talk about it if you want." Or, "Your classmate won the contest and you're feeling disappointed and jealous. That's OK. We all feel like that sometimes. Is there anything you would like to share about it?"

If we take away the negative messages about the shadow, it creates a safe space for children to explore their shadows and learn from them. It stops that generations-old practice of raising children to disconnect from their core selves.

If, up until now, you've been on a path of shadow denial and you want to change that with your children, here's a script for you: "I've been teaching you that some feelings are bad and that you shouldn't have them. I've learned I was wrong. It's important to take control of how we respond to our feelings, *and* it's perfectly OK to have those feelings. I'm going to work on this in myself and start helping you to accept your feelings too. All feelings are natural and normal, never bad. If you have any difficult feelings or thoughts that you want to talk about, I'm here. I am listening."

When my son was five, I took him and his friend on a hike. Halfway through, they were tired, discouraged, and ready to give up. I told them that it was okay to feel that way. It was a big hike, after all. We sat down, had some snacks, and I played a relaxing meditation. After fifteen minutes they felt recharged and ready to go. A few days later, I told my son I was feeling stressed. He went to my phone, put on my meditation app, and said, "Mom, this will help you relax." I laughed so much. Joyfully. He kept doing this every time I got stressed.

Welcome Your Shadow with Ceremony

We now come to one of my favorite concepts: If you want something different, you must *do* something different.

When it comes to things like our inner shadow—things that have been reinforced in us since the very start of our lives and from many different sources—turning that around for ourselves can be tricky. We're disrupting habits that are as deeply ingrained as walking and talking. I strongly believe that to make these shifts happen within ourselves, powerful practices outside ourselves can help solidify the new path we're trying to forge.

All over the world, there are cultures that have practiced ritual sacrifice as a means of carrying the shadow of the community. Whether in the form of food or luxuries, animal sacrifice, or even human sacrifice, we humans have a long history of creating rituals to mark emotionally momentous occasions and processes.

Ritual is important, but many existing rituals focus on projecting the shadow onto something else instead of accepting it within ourselves. Even in the rituals that acknowledge the shadow in the person, there's still this idea that the shadow is wrong and that we should turn our backs on it. It's time we start using the power of ritual to flip that on its head. Many of the rituals I've adopted came from my training with The Four Winds Society, but there are so many resources out there to inspire you. Often, all it takes is a Google search. Just be mindful of what resonates with you and respectful of the cultural origins of any rituals you explore. I challenge you to create or adopt a ceremony for yourself that calls up all parts of yourself with uncompromising love and acceptance and empowers you to release strong emotions once you've heard their message.

Our brains register ceremony as something transformative and meaningful. When we get married, there is a ceremony. When a loved one dies, there is a ceremony. Birthdays, baby showers, graduations, and housewarmings all have an element of ceremony, and for millennia humans have used ceremony to welcome the changing of the seasons. I find fire ceremonies to be a powerful practice. Fire is a transformative element and has been incorporated into the rituals of many cultures throughout time. There's the involvement of all our senses, the way it seems to reduce matter to nothing but ash, and that sense of being connected to generations of humans before us. When we use a fire ceremony and treat it with reverence, our brains register that shift.

I started practicing fire ceremonies to shift strong, difficult emotions, and now practice daily as part of my pre-work routine so that I can be at my best for my clients. It helps me feel active in letting go of the old and welcoming in something new and better. The ceremony can also be used to connect with and accept your shadow. Through the ceremony, you can burn the notion that any part of You needs to be suppressed. Burn the rug (symbolically, not an actual rug) you've been sweeping your shadow under, and welcome your shadow back home with love and acceptance.

If you have a fireplace or outdoor fire pit, you can use that. Otherwise, you can use a fireproof pot on a safe surface. Ensure you are near a water source or fire extinguisher.

Once you have your fire element, here's what you do:

Take a deep breath. Call in your guides, the Universe, or whatever higher force you believe in, and ask them to accompany you and help you welcome your shadow with love.

Take a piece of paper and write out the thoughts or feelings that have held You in your shadow. Alternatively, you can let yourself feel the intensity of whatever is holding you back, then blow it into the paper, at least three times. You can either leave the paper as-is or fold it up. Instead of a paper, you may also choose to blow onto a small stick or toothpick.

NOTE: A fire ceremony is also a powerful way to shift negative or difficult emotions. If you are using it for this purpose, write out the name of the emotion and your accompanying thoughts and feelings or feel the intensity of them and blow them into the paper.

Gently drop the paper/stick/toothpick into your fire. As it burns and smoke begins to emerge, say three times, "I release you." Feel that release. Then, draw your hands toward the smoke (not the flame) and visualize your shadow coming into the light as those limiting thoughts and feelings fade away. See your shadow elements, in all their human beauty, entering your circle of love and acceptance. Welcome your shadow home, calling it in exactly as it is.

NOTE: If you are working to shift emotions, think about what you want to shift in your life. If you are feeling hurt, you might call in love. If you are burning fearful thoughts, you might call in trust. For stress, you might call in peace. Remember that emotions can be created within you, so you don't have to think about who or where the feeling might come from. Just call it in. Welcome it.

Draw your hand toward three points of your body: your pelvic area, your heart, and your forehead. Those are your three primary energy centers. At each point, consciously inhale love and acceptance for your whole, human self (*if shifting emotions, feel the energy of what you're bringing in—love, trust, peace, etc*).

When the fire has finished burning, and the smoke has dissipated, thank your guides, the Universe, and/or your higher force for being with you on this journey.

For me, burning is the quickest way to create inner shifts without skipping the necessary steps of inner work. It helps release old patterns and beliefs at a deep level, so I can heal. There's also something deeply transformative about bringing an inner experience out into the physical realm, allowing myself to expand the experience and strengthen it.

Some things take time to shift. The energy they embody might be very intense, or embedded in lifelong patterns you're working to break. Or it may be an emotion such as grief, which can be layered and complex, and sometimes needs to be experienced in different ways for its sharp edges to smooth out and become less jagged and raw. In the case of our shadows, we've spent a lifetime with the belief that these parts of ourselves are unworthy; it will take time and practice to fully step into self-worth and let those feelings go.

Because of this, it is perfectly normal if you need to repeat the ceremony several times along your path. How that plays out may depend on how you've suppressed your shadow over the years. If your feelings have been big, loud, and dominating your life, every time you perform the ceremony, it will remove another layer of intensity. If you've been bottling things up, holding yourself at a distance from your own emotions, the ceremony may weaken that bottle, allowing you to feel things more strongly each time. However, in either scenario, you will emerge from every ceremony with a sense of calm. A sense that you're moving in the right direction. I've learned that it can take up to thirty days (a full moon cycle) for a shift to fully sink in. Imagine it like the layers of an onion or the petals of a lotus flower unfolding. Just as a flower may need to unfurl one petal at a time, it's only natural that you may need to release emotional blockages one layer at a time. Every time you practice the ceremony, another layer will come away.

Within a short time, you will notice different possibilities showing up for you. You may even start to experience a sense of lightness in your body as healthy connections are made and your shadow rejoins your worthy and wonderful self. Be open to receiving what comes. It is You, becoming whole again.

I share this practice with clients from all levels and backgrounds, including senior executives in Fortune 100 companies. With each practice, the person feels such a huge sense of relief and lightness. Like any tool, the only way to know if it's right for you is to try it out.

Taking it a Step Further

Connecting with your shadow will also strengthen your connection to your leader within. It's all part of the holistic You. Anytime you strengthen one connection, other connections will emerge, grow, and revitalize.

After performing your shadow ritual, take a moment to connect with your leader within. What's coming up? Is your inner leader pointing you toward anything? Let whatever it is come into the light. Maybe it's something around your career, family, or life purpose. Or maybe it's pointing you toward something like taking drum lessons. Joining a softball league. Taking a trip. Signing up for volunteer work. Starting or joining a book club. Learning to paint. Rediscovering a favorite video game. Riding a bike.

Personal growth journeys don't have to be all poignancy and inner exploration. At a certain point, you need to get out there and live your life according to your own instincts. If a desire to play hockey or tennis is hiding in your shadow, bring it out! If you keep thinking things like, "I'm too old. I'm no good at sports. I'll look ridiculous. I should be doing something productive," those thoughts are the rug you've been sweeping things under. Burn those thoughts, then get out and play.

The Shadow in Others

When you start exploring your own shadow you will start having epiphanies about the people around you. You'll start to understand, on a visceral level, how their choices and behaviors have absolutely nothing to do with you but are instead rooted in unexplored terrain within themselves. As you practice accepting your own shadow, set the intention to accept the shadow in others as well.

Accept that the people around you will make mistakes. They will say and do things that seem hurtful to you but may not have anything to do with you.

When you accept that the people around you have shadows— shadows they may struggle with—you are better able to respond to them with courage, compassion, and authenticity, and show up as your whole, connected self. This can have a profound effect on others, showing them that you are a safe space for shadows to be brought forward.

Acceptance also makes collaboration easier and helps you navigate conflict from a perspective of co-creation rather than right and wrong. When you accept the shadow as simply human, it's OK for someone to disagree with you, to believe different things, or to have conflicting ideas. Their perspective is not threatening to you; it isn't something to defend against. If anything, it gives you an opportunity to try on a different lens for yourself and appreciate the vibrancy of the world. In your work life, accepting the shadow empowers you to embrace conflict and difficult conversations in a way that cultivates co-creation. In your personal life, accepting the shadow allows you to love more deeply and fully, accepting the people you truly care about for all that they are.

To be clear, when I say to accept the shadow in someone else, I do not mean to accept someone being unkind to you, limiting you, expecting you to be someone for them or anything that hurts you, physically or emotionally. Accepting the shadow in others should not lead you to accept demands that you compromise who you are. What I mean is that, in the same way you accept your own complexities—the areas you need to grow, the times you are not perfect, the aspects of yourself that exist outside the status quo—accept that same complexity in others.

Maintain your boundaries, and do so with compassion. In fact, accepting someone exactly as they are may mean cutting them out of your life or setting even stronger boundaries. That's OK. Healthy boundaries are an act of love. How others react to your boundaries reflects their own journey. Accept it. Send them love. And continue on your path.

CEO of Your Life Coaching Tip:

Your shadow is part of You and is worthy of full acceptance. As you practice accepting your own shadow, set the intention to accept the shadow in others as well. Accept that the people around you will make mistakes. They will say and do things that seem hurtful to you but may not have anything to do with you. You can set healthy boundaries around hurtful behavior AND respect the person on the other side.

Create New Rituals and Habits

Whether you practice them consciously or not, your life is filled with regular habits and rituals that hold you where you are. Consciously creating new ones is a vital part of taking authorship of your life. It's where you start to put theory into action.

I once heard a story about a woman who always cut the legs off her Christmas turkey before roasting it. When asked why, she admitted she didn't really know, but it was how she'd been taught. She asked her mother, from whom she'd learned the technique, what was so important about removing the bird's legs before cooking. Her mother's response was that their old oven hadn't been big enough for a large turkey, so the legs were cooked separately!

Growing up, we integrate habits, rituals, and practices learned—through instruction or observation—from the people around us. And there's nothing wrong with that. Where it becomes a problem is when those habits, rituals, and practices are unhealthy. When they hold us back. When they make us afraid to try something new.

To add to this mix, some of those habits, rituals, and practices may not even have been taught to us. We might have been *born* with them.

Research into the descendants of prisoners of war from the American Civil War suggests that some of the effects of trauma may have been passed down to their children and grandchildren through changes in epigenetics (which, simplified, is about how certain genes are expressed) (Cost, Yetter, and DeSomer, 2018). And that isn't the only study to suggest that trauma can be passed down. In an experiment involving mice, researchers were able to condition a fear of certain smells, which was then passed down to the offspring of those mice (Callaway, 2013). That research is still evolving, but one thing we can take from it today is that how we react to the world around us is not always conscious or intentional. And there's good news in that. Just as trauma and habit can shape us, we can harness that power to heal ourselves and *re*shape ourselves.

A huge part of this healing and reshaping begins with accepting everything in your shadow, without judgement or justification. If you struggle with anxious or fearful thoughts or unhealthy habits that are hard to break, you don't have to justify any of it. For all you know, it may have come from your great-great-grandparents. And just as trauma may have changed things for your ancestors, you have the power to shift that change once again and heal the wound. How powerful is that?

Trauma, whatever its origins, isn't your fault. But it is your responsibility to deal with its impact on you. Accept it with love. However you adapted was your body and mind's way of trying to keep you safe. Then begin consciously creating new habits, practices, and rituals around creating healthier connections within yourself. Mark Bonchek, founder and CEO of Shift Thinking, talks about the process of unlearning habits (and learning new ones) as a three-stage process: First, develop the motivation to create change. This can be the hardest stage, as it requires recognizing your limiting beliefs and coming face-to-face with your fears. Second, visualize the new habits or rituals you want to create. Third, ingrain the new way of thinking into your mindset. (Bonchek, 2016).

It's normal for something new to feel unnatural for a while. Remember that your inner leader can help you understand if it feels unnatural because it's wrong for you or simply because it's different.

Start With a Morning Ritual

For many years, I've maintained a personally sacred morning routine that includes meditation, visualization, stretching, journaling, and reading. Prioritizing this "charging up" time before emails, social media, text messages, news, or even the weather report is part of how I practice intentionality—choosing, before anything else can influence me, how I will show up and respond throughout the day. When it comes to mindfulness and intentionality, it's important to work it into your daily routine in a way that works for you. That said, I strongly recommend establishing a morning ritual of some kind. It doesn't have to be complex or lengthy: it can be as simple as taking a few slow breaths, reaching toward the sky on the inhale, and folding toward the floor on the exhale. Even five minutes will do.

We all know the expression, "woke up on the wrong side of the bed." This is what happens when we let the circumstances around us set the tone for our day. Starting each day with intention gives us the power to choose for ourselves.

However, even vital rituals require flexibility. My morning ritual worked for me for years. Then Covid hit. I am fortunate enough to be able to work from home, so continuing to coach and support my clients seemed like a manageable challenge.

However, I suddenly found myself with more clients needing support in managing the impact of Covid on their lives, both personally and professionally. They were coming to me with unprecedented levels of stress. Many companies were also turning to coaches to help manage the transition from office life to remote work. It was a sudden and massive need, without any time to prepare. I became overwhelmed. My established routine wasn't enough to keep me centered and fueled throughout the day. I began adding in stretching moments between Zoom calls, taking breaks to lie back on the floor with my feet on a chair, and spending more time in meditation, breathing into the chaos in order to create from it.

It wasn't enough.

The anxiety and fatigue kept coming up. I had taken on too much. I was trying to be conscious of my decision making, but there was always something unexpected throwing me off. All of my appliances broke down over the span of a few months. It started with the fridge. Every day, for six months, I would fill a picnic basket with ice to store food, assuming this would just be temporary—the parts, due to supply chain issues, were backordered—and any day now, I'd have my fridge back. Next it was the stove's turn. The burners just stopped working. That same week, the dishwasher gave up and retired.

The icing on the cake was the washing machine. A manufacturer's defect caused it to spin out of control, smash into a wall and burst open. I wasn't sure if I should call a service center or an exorcist. The dryer, in solidarity with the washer, refused to start.

At a time when the world was plunging into chaos and uncertainty, my own little world seemed to be coming apart at the seams. Literally. When would it end? When would I get my peace back?

I knew it was on me to create my own peace, and I knew I needed help.

A few years ago, at a friend's wedding, I was fortunate enough to meet Eden Clark, a medical medium and shaman, who has helped guide me to create peace more than once. Facing all that upheaval, I turned to Eden for guidance. We hopped on a Zoom call, and I poured it all out to her. The stress, the chaos, the challenges I was facing personally and professionally. Clients were coming to me depressed, desperate, overwhelmed, sick, and uncertain—as low as I had ever seen them. I asked Eden how I could strengthen myself so that I could be strong for others.

"Melissa," she told me, "your default programming is that you need to do everything on your own, that you can't depend on anyone. You are taking on too much, not connecting to the earth, and not allowing the Universe to support you."

Oh my. A wound I thought I had healed was still there, lurking beneath the surface.

I knew she was right. Her intuition has always been spot-on with me; in that moment, it was the truth I needed to hear. Immediately after the call, I went outside to connect with the earth.

I've never felt I could fully lean on someone without being disappointed. It's why I feel the need to not only do things on my own but do them "perfectly." It's an exhausting pattern and not an easy one to change. It takes continual work and support. Asking for help was a step in the right direction, and it pointed me to the next step. (Isn't it wonderful how, when we do what feels right, it so naturally brings us to the next right thing?) To fully heal, I needed to trust the Universe to support me. That meant getting out of my mind and trusting the invisible.

In Maslow's hierarchy of needs, the lower levels—the most basic requirements of human beings—are physiological and safety needs. If these are not met, you can't reach up to those deeper needs of love, self-esteem, and self-actualization. There's a common misconception that once you get those bottom levels sorted out, it's "all uphill from there," and that isn't always the case. Life and circumstances are constantly changing, which means shifts can be experienced and old wounds can be exposed. When you are overwhelmed or your life is in turmoil, it can help to look back at those needs, especially your safety and sense of security, to see what you need. For me, it was a sense of disconnection from the earth and the Universe that was at the root of my distress. I was feeling unsupported.

As I've learned throughout my journey, an established *and* flexible morning routine is a powerful tool in times of unmet needs. Whenever

I need to support myself, strengthen a connection, or make a shift, I know I can reach for my morning routine to put that need into practice.

Connecting With Myself Through Grounding, Oneness, and Growing Forward

My guide's advice to me was, "Sit down on the earth, your perineum to the ground, for at least ten minutes a day, weather permitting. Mother Earth is a generator. When your circuitry isn't plugged into the earth, you are not recharging it." This practice is called grounding.

People practice grounding in different ways. My guide's advice to me was a strategy involving the root chakra, but grounding can also be practiced by walking barefoot on the earth or lying down in the grass with your arms, legs, and head in direct contact with the earth. Theories about how it works range from the electrical energy in the earth, to the mindfulness of being in direct physical contact with nature, to the sense of reassurance that comes from connecting with something as enduring and supportive as solid ground. Grounding helps us connect to the invisible and to feel a sense of Oneness—a feeling of being connected to everything and, therefore, disconnected from nothing. Practicing grounding daily has helped me feel more supported, more trusting, and less overwhelmed. I am more secure in my attachment to the earth.

Dr. Alberto Villoldo, a medical anthropologist who studied healing practices in the Amazon, says, "Until you glimpse non-ordinary, invisible reality, your brain will remain biased toward doubting 'what's out there.' But, when you experience Oneness, the sense of separation dissolves, as you perceive yourself to be an inextricable part of the larger whole" (Villoldo 2019).

I've studied energetic practices through Dr. Villodo's Four Winds Society for a few years. What I've learned about Oneness is that it's an experience of balance between two levels or realms of being: the level of the mind and the level of the mythic.

The mind is your connection to the human-made world. The mythic is your connection to something greater. For me, that greater something is the Universe. For others, it's God, the spiritual world, or simply "a higher power." It's the invisible world. We can't see it directly, but we can sense it and experience its impact. You don't need to be religious or follow a belief system to experience the mythic. If you lean more toward science, you might look to quantum entanglement. As beings made up of matter and energy, we are connected to the wider universe in ways we may not yet fully understand, but we know that we're connected all the same (Emspak 2022).

The mind realm is your programming. It comes from family, education, friends, co-workers, romantic relationships, even social media. Building your career, raising your family, managing your household . . . it's all at the mind level.

The mythic is infinite and ageless. When you meditate, pray, dream, practice grounding, get lost in music, engage in an art form, connect with nature, tune into your inner GPS, and so on . . . all of this is the mythic. It's how you connect to the drumbeat of the Universe. Although the mythic is vast, it is also grounding. Working at the mythic level strengthens your connection to something greater, which is an antidote to feelings of disconnection.

When we experience a prolonged state of unease or unrest, it's usually the result of an imbalance between these two levels or realms. Without a firm foot in the mythic, the mind gives over to fear.

Consider the pandemic. That threw many of us fully into the mind level. We worried about our families, jobs, physical health, security, the availability of essential goods, and so on. All of that is essential to our survival. It mattered to keep a solid foot in that realm. Because we lost our footing in the mythic, many of us got caught in a prolonged, heightened state of anxiety and disconnection. Existing only in this chaotic, uncertain human-made world, we needed a grounding connection more than ever.

There was no guidebook for the pandemic. No clear map for how to navigate the "new normal" we were thrust into. When there is no staircase, we must build one. However, if we try to build anything in a heightened state of stress, it will be shaky and create even more chaos. We need firm footing in the mythic AND the mind to create something balanced, stable, and climbable.

For me, building that staircase meant really leaning into my mindfulness practices because mindfulness is like a gateway to the mythic. It meant extra time in meditation, taking "inversion breaks," and practicing grounding. It meant taking more time to recognize and accept my myriad emotions without needing to "fix" them. Step by step, my staircase was revealed, and that was all I needed. Just the next step, followed by the next, and so on.

One of those steps was to bring even more of my energetic practices into my coaching sessions. These practices were helping me, and I believed they would help my clients as well. I also felt that by bringing in more of that aspect of myself, I would be coaching with a more holistic approach that would keep me better connected to my full, authentic, worthy self. I recognized this step through the mythic, then leaned into my mind to guide the "how to" of carrying it out.

The pandemic is an extreme example, but we see this in so many areas. Something goes wrong at work and we go at it, full force, with just our minds. Stress skyrockets. We make judgements and rash decisions. We blame ourselves or others. There is no peace. No stable staircase. Or our children struggle at school, for example, and we start hiring tutors, beating ourselves up for failing as parents, admonishing our children for not studying hard enough, setting up teacher meetings, and extending homework time, all before taking a moment to connect with our higher knowledge.

What if, instead, we stopped and asked ourselves, "Where are both my feet right now?" Then did the work to re-establish balance, before trying to build our staircase?

Once I understood this need for balance, I realized that more than half of my clients were going through similar situations and that it was showing up in their personal and professional lives. I shared what I had learned with them and started receiving pictures of them grounding in all kinds of different ways and sceneries. It was a powerful way to create connection during such a disconnected time.

I gained a new motto from this: "Get your ass sitting on the grass." In winter, I even get my ass sitting in the snow with my snow pants on. I know that I may have to shift this practice one day, but I also know that, for now, I'm healing and strengthening my core self, which will help me continue to adapt and thrive through whatever the future brings.

Establish Nourishing Habits

Both healing and growth require nourishment. Just as we nourish our bodies, our minds and spirits need nourishment as well. Energy flows through everything. If you allow negative energy to take root in one area, it absolutely will flow into other areas. Feed your body, mind, and spirit with nourishing elements, and that positive energy will begin to flow as well.

Take a good look at how you fill your days. You might even try keeping a journal. Start with the time you wake up, and record how you spend each hour or segment of the day. You can include food and drink as well, but if that's an area you've struggled with, you may find just the act of keeping a journal to be draining. Feel free to leave that out.

Once you have a few days logged, go through your journal with two different color highlighters. Highlight the things that fuel you in one color and those that drain you in another. If you can't decide whether something is nourishing or draining, use the Light Method from Lesson One. For example, maybe you had an emotional phone call with a friend. It was intense, and you felt tired afterwards. But when you think back to it using the Light Method, your body is sending you feelings of lightness and warmth. You feel closer to your friend now that the call is over. It was nourishing!

On the other hand, maybe there was a lot of judgement or gossip. Maybe they brought up things from your past. Maybe they were in a victim mindset or using you as an emotional dumping ground. If you think back on it and feel heavy or feel discomfort in your body, that's a sign that it was a draining event.

Once you've gone through the journal with your highlighters, notice how much of your draining color is on there. Does it show up a lot? Is it concentrated in certain areas of your life, or spread out? Are there any surprises?

Next, go through everything one more time:

Look at your draining items. What can you cut out?

Look at your nourishing items. What can you do more of? How can you increase these nourishing events, activities, and relationships?

Don't feel the need to rush. Maybe commit to working on just one thing each week or even month. If you've been letting a lot of draining things fill up your life, there's a reason for that. As you start to change, difficult thoughts and feelings may come up. Give yourself the emotional space to let them come up. Explore them. Work through them. Then release them.

Nourish Your Body and Brain

Good nutrition is a basic, foundational need. It's only when we nourish ourselves well at a basic level that our higher-level selves can truly come forward. Through my training with the Four Winds Society, I've learned so much about how we, as humans, function, heal, adapt, survive, and thrive. One of my favorite lessons is the concept of the four brains (Villoldo 2019).

Reptilian brain: Your survival brain keeps your heart beating, lungs expanding, and all the other basic functions that our brains handle without us having to be conscious of it.

Mammalian brain: Where your primal drives, your "Four F's" (fear/fleeing, fighting, feeding, and fornicating), live. What else happens here? Emotions. Our primal needs are tied to anger, joy, fear, and comfort so that we can be pushed into action.

Neocortex: Creativity lives here, which is not just art but also problem solving, innovation, math, imagination, and so on. Where your mammalian brain might say "RUN," your neocortex might say, "What else is possible here?"

Prefrontal cortex: Executive functioning lives here. This brain ties everything together, empowering you to calm reactive impulses and tap into creativity. It allows you to stay focused on big picture outcomes to avoid short-sighted, knee-jerk reactions. Even better, you can purposefully strengthen this brain through mindfulness and meditation.

What does this concept of the four brains have to do with nutrition? Although research is still in early stages, it is starting to suggest that what we eat plays a role in how our brains function as a whole (Selhub 2020). For example, we know that a high-sugar diet can wreak havoc on brain function and make it harder to access the calming influence of the prefrontal cortex (Rivera 2020). We also have plenty of anecdotal evidence of people (myself included) saying their minds feel clearer when they start eating a more nourishing diet and cutting out highly processed foods. Overall, good nutrition is a key element of good energy and the ability to bring our best selves forward. When you eat healthy, your gut is clear, which helps increase your inner connection and intuition (Robertson 2020). There's a reason intuition is often called a "gut feeling."

For me, I stopped eating wheat, dairy, sugar, and red meat (with some exceptions on special occasions). My body now feels a lot healthier, which means I feel better, have more energy, and think more clearly. This way of eating might not appeal to everyone, but it works for me. For you, it may help to focus on what you want to add to your diet instead of what to take away. For example, eating healthy fats or incorporating more veggies.

Consider how you nourish your body and think about what you can shift or eliminate to help increase your energy and clarity of mind. Work mindfulness into your diet by appreciating what you give to your body and brain when you eat. Take a moment at meal and snack times to marvel at what the Universe has gifted us. Try new things to find what works and lean into curiosity. Whenever something does or does not feel right, notice what comes up and ask, "What thoughts and feelings are coming up that I might need to work through?"

Like anything else, you can start small. Maybe an apple a day. It may seem negligible, but eating in a way that nourishes you will fuel you in a deeply impactful way. Maybe for you, it's not an apple but a banana. Or swapping soda for tea, or coffee for matcha. Take it one step at a time. Forgive and love yourself for setbacks. This isn't about weight, looks, or other people's opinions. It's about nourishing yourself in the way that wonderful, amazing You deserves.

Oh, Fertilizer!

As Fred Kofman, leadership development advisor for Google and founder of the Conscious Business Center International, says, "Instead of saying 'Oh shit, why is this happening to me?' Try, 'Oh fertilizer! How can this make me grow?'" For me, the fertilizer in the chaos of the pandemic was learning how to stay calm, stay grounded, and care for myself emotionally and nutritionally during a seemingly unending storm.

Let's face it. It's easy to stay calm when the world around you is calm. It can even feel easy to stay calm in chaos, so long as you can see the way through. But how do you bring that calm into times of uncertainty and disconnection? For me, the answer is grounding, feeling Oneness, practicing an energizing morning routine, and eating healthy foods that nourish and fuel me. This is how I hold myself in a state of connection and security, empowering me to continually work toward greater self-actualization, always creating from what's happening around me.

Everyone's path to connection is unique to them, but there are frameworks that can be used by anyone to create their unique path. These are things like good morning routines, healthy habits, and mindfulness practices that align with the energy you want to create.

No matter where you are today, healing empowers you to grow forward. When a stem is cut from a plant, the wound left behind is vulnerable. But, if it's able to heal, new and lush growth can emerge from the healed wound. Your wounds do not have to be an end. They can also be a source of new beginnings.

CEO of Your Life Coaching Tip:

Life is in the details. Commit to becoming conscious of the rituals, habits, and practices holding you where you are today and consciously creating new ones that nourish You. Work on your energy. Try different things until you find what works for you. Recognize your wounds and embrace them with love and acceptance. Give your body what it needs. Refuel in nature. Eat healthy foods to help you show up as your best self. Above all, put yourself in charge of how you show up every day.

Tune Into Your Body

Did you know that the body sends about eleven million pieces of information per second to the brain for processing (DiSalvo 2013)?

Yet the conscious mind can only process forty bits per second. With all that information coming in, how are we only consciously aware of such a miniscule percentage? When you think about it, our nervous system does so much for us—from spatial awareness to temperature changes to visual input. Imagine if we were fully conscious of every single piece of information. We wouldn't be able to function!

However, within those millions of inputs resides valuable knowledge. Information that can help us make better decisions and better understand the world around and within us. This wisdom is your bridge to the life around you. A critical part of self-leadership is tapping into the messages of your body and understanding how to use them cohesively with your logical brain. These messages *are* coming in and *will* impact your state of mind and how you show up. The choice is yours: do you let yourself be passively influenced, or will you tune into your body's wisdom, learn from it, and make conscious decisions about how you respond?

Our Brain-Centric Legacy

Throughout history, humans have had different ideas about where we do our thinking. Some believed it was in the heart while others thought that it originated in the gut. As our knowledge evolved, we realized a lot was happening in the brain, and that became our understanding of the center of all thought and behavior.

Philip Shepherd, founder of The Embodied Present Process (TEPP), writes in his book, *The Embodiment Manifesto*, "Today it is . . . understood that the head is the center of the psyche, and that every aspect of the self—our thoughts, our emotions, our desires and senses—is held in orbit by what lies within our cranium" (Shepherd 2017). He then goes on to outline what neuroscientists and researchers have discovered as their understanding of consciousness continues to evolve—our thoughts, emotions, desires, senses, and more are a result of processes that occur throughout the body. For example, we now know that roughly half a billion neurons reside within the human digestive system, leading to a strong connection between what happens in the gut and our emotional well-being (Underwood 2018). In her groundbreaking book *Beyond Behaviors*, Dr. Mona Delahooke explores the fascinating concept of what she refers to as top-down and bottom-up behaviors (Delahooke 2019). Contrary to widely held beliefs, Dr. Delahooke asserts that our behaviors don't all originate in our brains but can originate within our bodies.

From a scientific perspective, research is (excitingly) ongoing. However, what we can take from this and put into practice right now is that our bodies and brains are meant to work together far more holistically than our society has encouraged. In fact, our society has been encouraging brain-body disconnection far more than anything else.

Think of every product, service, practice, and habit that only serves to keep us further disconnected from our thoughts and feelings. We indulge in alcohol to avoid sitting with our feelings, use food to stave off boredom, binge watch television instead of seeking true fulfillment, and buy things to treat the symptoms of our emotional wounds instead of exploring and healing their root causes. So many of us keep ourselves constantly busy and engage in reflexive consumption to "fill a void" when the liberating truth is that the void does not exist. The real issue is disconnection. We train ourselves to disconnect our logical brains from what we're feeling in our bodies, but our brains and bodies are parts of a whole system that are meant to work together.

If our habit, for example, is not to sit with our difficult feelings but to try and shove them aside, it makes sense that we'd feel like something is missing and that we'd look outside ourselves to address that feeling. For me, I often felt like I wasn't good enough to be fully loved just as I was. I avoided sitting with that feeling; it was something I hadn't really articulated, so figuring out how to address it in a healthy way was out of reach. I just knew something was missing. For years, I tried to fill that gap—what felt like a void—with external achievements and relationships. I had it in my head that if my life looked a certain way, I would feel whole. It really wasn't until I started my coaching journey that I understood the void as a disconnection. When I started connecting with what I felt in my body, getting that in sync with what I thought in my mind, getting clarity, step-by-step, on the roots of the feeling, learning to love myself, and practicing being with the feelings and allowing them to move on . . . that's when I started to experience a sense of wholeness. Inner connection helped the void feel smaller.

It's no wonder so many of us feel lost, stuck, or directionless. We have purposely fragmented ourselves. To feel whole again, we need to heal that disconnection. We need to intentionally tune back into our bodies and make that a regular practice until it becomes our natural state of being.

Here are some examples of what tuning into your body can look like:

Notice the butterflies in your stomach before a big meeting: Are they fear, anxiety, excitement? A mix?

Your shoulders tense up when someone walks into the room: Who is this person to you? What's your history with them? What do they represent for you?

You feel a sluggish feeling throughout your body, and all medical reasons have been ruled out: Where and when do you feel it most? What emotions is it connected to?

Your heart is racing, but there is no immediate danger around you: What is different in your life right now? What's changed or might soon change?

Your body feels light and agile during a task: What are you enjoying about this task? What does it mean for you? How can you do more of this?

The Body's Knowledge

When I was a kid, certain people just gave me bad vibes. I couldn't put it into words; sometimes I felt they were cold or being around them would make me uncomfortable. I would start to close up or just get bad feelings in my body. It was always a very physical feeling of just *knowing* something was off.

As I grew up, I started to ignore those feelings. I was taught to be polite and do what was expected, so I pushed aside what my intuition was telling me in order to do "what was right." When those feelings came up, my mind would just tell me there must be something wrong with me. Today, I know that my childhood instincts were right. But even in early adulthood, I was still ignoring those messages, even though my body was shouting them loudly.

Someone once saw a video of me at a dinner with some negative people. This person told me that my whole personality and even body posture changed. I knew I wasn't comfortable at that dinner, but I didn't realize it was affecting me so physically. Those people were sucking the life out of me, and my body knew it.

That video made it all click for me. My body was trying to pull me away from people it knew were wrong for me, and my brain wouldn't listen. This old programming in my brain insisted that I show up for others, ignore my gut instincts, and shove them into the shadow where all the other wrong parts of myself had to stay. It had created blockages in my mind-body-spirit connections, and I was suffering for it.

You might pick up on a negative vibe. You might get a spasm in your stomach, feel a nervous twitch, or find yourself lost for words. Your mouth might go dry, and your palms may sweat; you might feel your energy dropping or, conversely, feel anxiety or palpitations; you may feel your body temperature change. Your muscles may knot and tense, or your shoulders might rise and come forward as if your body is trying to roll in on itself. And you are probably in the habit of ignoring or explaining away those reactions.

STOP.

Whatever you are feeling in your body, ask your body, "What are you trying to tell me?" Your body is using these signals to try and make you listen to yourself. When we ignore those signals, we start to feel sick, anxious, overwhelmed, or stuck. Our bodies have a unique and powerful way of telling us when a person, place, or situation is not good for us. If we tune into our bodies and trust the warnings, we can avoid a lot of hurt and frustration. Work with your body, rather than fighting against it.

Below are five steps to help you reconnect with your body's messages. Although I've laid them out as consecutive steps, you can lean into any one (or more) of these steps at any time, depending on what you need in the moment.

Five Steps to Tune into Your Body

Step One: Consciously tune into your gut.

We are so accustomed to ignoring our bodies' messages that we need to make a conscious plan to break the habit. Start each day with the clear intention to tune into what your body is saying. You may want to put a note by your bed, where you'll see it first thing in the morning, that says, "Body, how are you feeling?" Or you can set up cues for yourself throughout the day. Maybe every time you pass through a doorway or encounter a new person, you take a few seconds to become aware of any new feelings in your body. Maybe it's a string tied around your wrist, and every time you notice it, you take a second to assess what's happening in your body and how it might relate to what's happening around you. Whatever works for you. The more you practice this—intentionally—the sooner it will become an ingrained habit.

Step Two: Assess your environment.

It's easy to say you should ignore external influences, but external influences do have a lot of, well, influence. What gets repeated gets remembered and becomes part of our world. When we're exposed to certain images, ideas, and expectations on a regular basis, they will have an impact. Yes, there's a lot in the world we cannot control. Turn your focus to what you can control.

Make a list of all the places you go, activities you engage in, and people you meet with. Think about work, home, family, social networks, clubs, your kid's sporting events, the grocery store, friends, volunteering, medical professionals, your gym . . .

Do any of these places, people, or activities set something off in you? Just the act of writing them down may start to spark a sensation in your body. Keep in mind that positive associations are just as important to recognize as negative ones, so make note of those as well.

Ask yourself, "What about this person/place/activity is causing this feeling? What is my body trying to tell me?" You might come to realize that your neck pain at the office has nothing to do with the ergonomics of your chair and everything to do with a new manager or project. You might realize that regular doctor's visits for a health issue are causing emotional distress and you need additional support. Or you might realize a family member, friend, or romantic partner you keep telling yourself is just a bit difficult is much more toxic than that.

You can control much of the media you consume, the people you spend your time with, the physical space you live in, and so on. You can also control your approach to these things. If you have a boss or colleague who is unkind to you, for example, but you aren't able to leave your job, you can choose to repeat a mantra to yourself when you interact with them. Something like, "I know I don't deserve this, and their behavior says more about them than it does about me. I am worthy of better." No, it does not solve the root problem. It does, however, address those feelings in your body in a way that reinforces your inherent worth as a human being.

Step Three: Learn the difference between intuition and Saboteurs.

We all have negative voices in our heads. Voices that say things like, "You can't do that. You're wrong. Who do you think you are?" In coaching, we call these voices Saboteurs, and they are the keepers of our shadow gates. They fear change. They try to keep us safe by maintaining the status quo. Saboteurs are to be given love and compassion, then promptly ignored.

How do you tell the difference between intuition and Saboteurs? Intuition guides you. Saboteurs freeze you. Your body will tell you the difference. Take a deep breath and think about the person, situation, or decision you are faced with. Visualize yourself moving forward. What is your body telling you? Does it feel light, relaxed, or maybe even excited or fired up? Or does it feel heavy? Do you feel a sharp pain, tightness, or discomfort? Your body knows. Tune into it.

Step Four: Get comfortable with no explanation.

Intuition or "gut feeling" is just that. A feeling. We often don't have any "hard evidence" of someone else's bad intentions. You may not be able to explain exactly why something or someone feels wrong to you. You do not need to justify or explain your feelings to anyone. Get comfortable with not always having a "logical" explanation. When your body shouts "GET AWAY," listen to it.

Step Five: Stay alert to red flags.

This is especially important when it's a person your body is warning you against. Negative or toxic people continuously put spikes in your wheel. They either find fault, are unsupportive, or just plain drain you with their drama. They usually don't care what you want or what is important to you. Everything they do is about feeling better about themselves. If a person doesn't respect you, your feelings, or your boundaries, that's a huge red flag.

Does this person consistently place blame but rarely take responsibility? Do they regularly put down your ideas or feelings or flat out ignore them? Do they often overstep your boundaries and refuse to take "no" for an answer? Do they always seem to need you but are never available when you need something? These are all red flags that your head may not be attuned to, but your body is. When your body sends you a warning message, look for the red flag. With time, you'll be able to notice these red flags in people before you get too involved.

Tuning into your body is just another way of turning to your leader within. Leaning into the Light Method, in combination with a regular meditation practice, can really help you explore and understand what your body is telling you, giving you a clearer understanding of your inner experience so that you can then consciously respond to it rather than simply reacting moment to moment.

When faced with different choices or uncomfortable situations, take a moment to really feel each possibility. Visualize yourself following through with each path and feel the energy of it in your body. With many decisions, it's simply a matter of feeling that "light" path within your body. That is often the path most aligned with You.

That said, when something feels heavy or uncomfortable, it's so important to explore why.

Taking the Light Method a Step Further

Sometimes you'll try the Light Method, but the feelings aren't so straightforward. In this case, get curious about what's behind the heavy feelings. Is it something you fear that you need to face? Is it a wound that needs healing? Is it a challenging path with a lot of murky mud to get through before finding solid ground?

Some paths may feel heavy but need to be taken to empower growth. Try visualizing the outcome—how you will feel or how your life will look after you've moved through this challenge. If that outcome feels light, that's probably a path you need to explore.

Let's say the idea of quitting your job feels heavy. Telling your boss will be uncomfortable. You feel afraid of trying to find something else that pays well. The interview process is unnerving, and you find yourself intimidated by the unknown. That's the mud, and mud can weigh you down. Instead, visualize how you will feel in a new role that has everything you want in a career—an environment you love and a feeling of being respected, seen, appreciated, and surrounded by colleagues you enjoy collaborating with. How does that feel? Chances are it's worth the mud. Facing your fears will help you grow and discover new strengths within yourself.

On the flip side, visualizing the outcome of a path that feels light is also important. In the example above, the immediate path of staying in your current role may feel lighter, but spending the next several years in an unfulfilling role may weigh heavily in your body.

If you need to, partner with a mentor, coach, or therapist to help. Reconnecting with yourself is a powerful experience. It isn't easy, and taking real steps toward living that connection can feel scary. Having a guide along the way can help you stay accountable for taking action, mirror back to you what's coming up in the moment, and give you tools and practices that empower you to continually maintain and strengthen your brain-body connection as you go.

CEO of Your Life Coaching Tip:

The wisdom in your body is your bridge to life around you and your path to healing the fragmentation of mind and body. Don't ignore or discredit the messages your body is telling you. They are coming up for a reason and deserve your attention. Meditation is a practice that guides us to reconnect our bodies and minds with intention. Consider trying a few different approaches to meditation to see if there is a good fit for you.

Cultivate a Flexible Vision and Purpose

Trying to live up to externally imposed expectations, rather than living as You, is exhausting. We all know that trying to live up to celebrity standards, cultivated social media personas, or even that friend who always seems to have it together isn't emotionally healthy. However, this tendency can be much broader, going right back to the very beginning of our lives, and be so ingrained that we aren't even fully aware we're doing it.

As children, we absorb the values of those around us and internalize the practice of living up to something outside of ourselves. We're given a set of beliefs and expectations by the adults around us rather than encouraged to develop those things for ourselves. This process is not always a bad thing: it's natural for families and communities to pass their values down to younger generations. When that helps you to love, honor, and grow yourself, that's a wonderful thing. But when those values don't work for you, leave you feeling guilty, bog you down with the sensation of always falling short, or make you feel like you must put on a facade to be accepted, it is time to ask whether those values are truly serving you.

Your Purpose

Having a purpose is like having a guiding star that works in tandem with your leader within. It helps you continually align your choices with the life you want to create for yourself. Often, when people talk about having purpose, they talk about big, monumental goals like ending hunger or curing an illness. These are awe-inspiring objectives, but our purpose doesn't need to be that big or outward-facing. In fact, one of the most impactful ways we can change the world around us is to simply be our best and most authentic selves. That means determining a purpose that truly resonates with you.

A life purpose (one that truly resonates with you and aligns with your core values) builds your confidence and resilience and empowers better long- and short-term decision making. When you have a clear purpose and have made a habit of consciously aligning with it, you are more likely to be persistent and focused in moving towards big picture objectives and are more likely to make decisions that serve the long view for yourself and your work. The first thing to know is that a purpose is not final. It's not about your *whole* life but about your life as it is today. As you grow and evolve, it's natural and healthy for your purpose to grow and evolve as well. Don't get too hung up on getting your purpose exactly right the first time around. Get to something that feels right to You in this chapter of your life.

How do you determine your purpose? It's all about asking yourself deep questions that get to the heart of what matters to You. I recommend doing this with a coach, as they will pick up on things you might miss, act as a sounding board to help you get the clearest picture possible, and guide you through any feelings of being stuck. Here are a few questions I share with clients I am coaching in order to get them started:

When do I feel I am at my best? When do I feel like I am having a positive impact? If I had to share my biggest life lesson, what would it be? If I had the opportunity to create a brand-new planet, what would it look like? What role would I like to play in it?

Be as raw and honest as possible in your answers. Get vulnerable with yourself. Set aside time to really sit with, and dig into, the questions that stir something in you.

The next step is to start drafting variations of a life purpose statement for yourself. You can use whatever form you like, but if you're stuck on where to start, try this formula: "I am the (metaphor) _____ that/who (impact) _____." This formula paints a picture of how you see your best self and how you want to bring that out into the world. My life purpose statement, for example, is, "I am a fresh burst of uniqueness that inspires you to step into your light!"

Whatever your statement, it must make sense for YOU.

Once you have a draft that feels good to you, try it out with people you trust—people who you feel in your heart want you to create joy in your life, however that may look. If you don't have anyone like this, consider a coach, therapist, healer, or someone else who has made it *their* life purpose to help others. You could also try reading your statement out loud to yourself in the mirror. Speaking out loud allows us to connect with our words in a more visceral way, feeling them with our whole selves, instead of just mulling them over in our minds. As you repeat your statement to different people or in different ways, how does it begin to evolve?

The Evolution of My Purpose Statement

Six years after I was first asked to determine my purpose, I found myself in a new leadership program being asked to state my purpose again. My previous purpose, one I determined early in my coaching journey, had served me at the time, but it wasn't me anymore. I struggled to determine a purpose that resonated with the person I was becoming. I asked myself all the questions I typically pose to clients.

And I was stuck.

That's when one of my leaders asked, "What was one of the most painful things to happen to you in your life?"

Wow. I thought hard. I felt strong emotions emerging, which was scary but also meant something important was being excavated. I realized that a recurring pattern throughout my life has been the feeling that I could never be accepted for the true person I am. It has always been a source of deep hurt.

However, the difference in this new chapter of my life was that I had come to terms with people not accepting the true me. I knew that the right people did accept me, and that's what mattered. With that realization, I started playing with different versions of my new life purpose.

My first draft was, "I am the joyful lightworker who illuminates the leader within you, guiding you to bring it forward, bravely and unapologetically, in your work, home, and community." My homework was to say it out loud to ten different people and see how it evolved. As I did, I could sense in my body what felt good and what needed tweaking. I heard people's feedback of what they felt was me and what wasn't.

During that process, it evolved into, "I am the joyful lightworker who empowers you to bring your true self forward, bravely and unapologetically, no matter where you are or who you are with."

I shared that statement with Michael Wallace, an amazing coaching colleague, who said, "I believe the statement needs to be short, and it needs to punch me in the face—or at least slap me on the ass." What a guy!

I refined my statement further: "I am the lightworker that empowers you to be you, no apologies." I then shared it with my tribe members in the leadership program. They felt it was good, but they saw me as a very energetic person and felt the statement was missing a bit of energizing, eccentric, quirky Melissa-ness.

So we played with two more variations:

"I am the burst of light that energizes you to be you, no apologies," and "I am the quirky surge that energizes you to be you, no apologies."

For days I repeated them both out loud, seeing what resonated most in my body, but it wasn't quite a punch in the face. I started to think about what lit me up at my core. One thing is shamanic energy medicine, which is based on the idea that everything in the Universe is made of light. The more luminous we are, the healthier we are, and the more we create the script we want to live.

I kept meditating on my purpose until it came to me: I had worked hard to bring my own light forward. I felt luminous, and I wanted to bring that luminous feeling to others. Beyond that, I knew I wanted to do it in my own unique way. A fresh new way. I wanted to be a *burst* of freshness for people feeling stuck in old patterns or weighed down by the heaviness of the world around them.

I knew, without a doubt, I had it!

And so . . . "I am a fresh burst of uniqueness that inspires you to step into your light!"

That feels so incredible to write down and even better to say out loud. It's so totally me! Once you can say your life purpose out loud and feel it resonate as truly part of You, reflective of You, Your truth, and Your most amazing self, it's time to start bringing it forward into the world.

Bringing Your Purpose Forward

A purpose is more than a statement. It's a personal call to action. Ask yourself, "What is a quest I could take on, personally or professionally, where I can bring my life purpose forward?" Focus on what is possible from where you are, right now.

Here are some of the quests that grew out of my life purpose that I have been working toward:

Publishing this book and incorporating the lessons here into keynotes and workshops to help guide people worldwide on bringing their true selves forward, no matter where they are, who they are with, or what they do.

Continuing to work on my inner connection, setting healthy boundaries, and cutting out toxic people. I will evolve this balance on a personal level and guide others on how to find and evolve their own balance.

Sharing coaching tools in schools so that children can learn empowering coaching techniques at an early age and use them to strengthen their sense of self, understand and practice self-love, and expand their decision-making skills, equipping them to succeed in their educations, careers, relationships, and other aspects of their lives.

These three quests translate my purpose into actionable goals that can be broken down into real steps. That's what authenticity truly is: acting on your internal purpose in your external life. Tune into your statement daily. It's the energy you want to show up in the world with. I say it as part of my morning ritual, starting each day with intentional energy. Imagine saying your purpose before a meeting or an important conversation. What impact would it have? Knowing and tuning into your purpose gives you an extra dose of strength and confidence. The people around you will feel this strength. Although they may not be able to put their finger on what they're sensing, the impact will be felt. In this way, showing up with the energy of your purpose is extremely powerful.

Your Vision

Create a vision of the life you ultimately want for yourself. One that also works for your life today and will evolve along with you.

Start by getting clear on where you are. There's a simple, effective coaching tool called a personal assessment wheel (also called a wheel of life or balance wheel). Inspired by my coach training at CTI, I divide it into nine key areas: career, fun & recreation, money & finances, physical environment, personal growth, health & wellbeing, friends, family, and significant other. You can download a printable worksheet from my website or, if you prefer, simply get a blank piece of paper, draw a circle, and divide it into nine sections. It doesn't have to be perfect.

Your task is to fill in how fulfilled you feel in each area at this point in your life. This will give you a powerful visual into what's working and not working. It will show you the strengths you can build on and lean into for support, as well as areas to work on and areas where you need to be kind with yourself.

Connect with What Feels Right for You

We all carry beliefs about who or what we "should" be. There's nothing wrong with these beliefs when they feel right in your heart. Where they become a problem is when they aren't right for you.

As much as you may want to gain approval, live up to an ideal, or be accepted, seeking external validation puts your energy in someone else's hands. That's a resource you cannot regulate or renew. When you instead connect with what truly feels right to you, you become the keeper of your own validation and energy.

Taking it to the next step, ask yourself, "If I felt completely fulfilled by each area of my assessment wheel, what would it look like? If I had a magic wand, what would I make possible?" Limiting ourselves is so habitual that it is important to adopt the mindset that "everything is possible." Completely remove those limits in your mind and let yourself imagine it all.

As you consider each area, feel your answers in your body. Assume the energy of your ideal life as if you are living it today. Create a full vision in your mind of this life you want to work toward. Don't let limiting thoughts or beliefs derail this vision. Tap into your shadow and your leader within. Let them guide your imagination as it weaves a picture for you.

A Vision Board as a Blueprint

It's one thing to visualize something in your mind and quite another to make it happen. A vision board helps you shape your vision. It externally manifests what you want to create. What gets repeated gets remembered and becomes your world. Vision boards are like blueprints that help you hone your focus, empowering you to make decisions that bring you closer to what you want. They keep you engaged in the unfolding of your story, rather than being a bystander, with people and circumstances around you pushing and pulling your life in different directions.

If you, like me, spent years holding a vision for your life that wasn't truly You, it will take time and deliberate action to start holding a new vision of what's possible. It may take time to fully believe, with your whole self, that your vision is possible. A vision board helps with that repetition. You can create a digital or physical board: if you choose a physical board, I recommend something like a cork board and push-pins so that you can easily modify it if the need arises.

Put your life purpose statement on the board, then fill it with images that align with your values, purpose, and vision. Include a unique image for each of the life areas you imagined in the magic wand question above. This could be pictures of people, scenery, meaningful items or spaces, animals, artwork—anything that speaks strongly to your purpose and vision. You may include color schemes, drawings, quotes, song lyrics, people who inspire you, things you feel proud of and want to carry forward. Take your time with it, remembering that this too is meant to evolve. You can also include pictures of things in your life right now that are going well and you want to maintain.

Tune into your vision board daily. When you do so, you are tapping into Future You: the you that you are working toward being. Tap into that energy. Ask yourself, "If this was in my life right now, what would I say? What would I do? How would I answer the questions I am asking myself right now?"

Aim to make decisions from the perspective of Future You. Anytime you feel stuck, use your vision board to tap into that energy. Ask Future You what they did to get to where they are. When torn between different paths, which path aligns best with Future You? This is what vision boards are about: having a visual anchor to the future you want to create. If you're a scheduler, sit with your vision board when planning your day, week, or month. Are the items you're scheduling aligned with your vision? Are you scheduling at least one step each week that brings you closer to your vision?

Put your vision board somewhere accessible. Commit to taking at least ninety seconds a day to sit with your vision, allowing yourself to feel the energy of that ideal life. This empowers you to go out with intention, focused on taking real steps forward, and tuned into opportunities around you.

Have you ever learned a new word or concept and suddenly, you start seeing it all around you? It was always there: you're just attuned to it now, and so you notice when it appears. It's the same with opportunities. When you take the time to tune yourself in, every day, you will suddenly start to see opportunities that were always there and recognize new ones as they come up.

Cultivate Your Environment

Whether you're aware of it or not, your current environment is likely filled with visual reminders of old habits and limiting beliefs. When you are intentional about cultivating the environment around you, you get to decide what influences you.

When I think about creating or organizing a space, I think of Marie Kondo's advice to look for things that "spark joy" (Kondo 2012). Focus on things that spark joy, inspiration, acceptance, and unconditional love for yourself.

Not all of us can afford to completely redecorate our work and living spaces, and you may not need to either. What you can do is let go of things that feel anchored to the old life you want to leave behind. Display items that inspire feelings of hope, courage, compassion, love, or whatever you want to draw in. Curate corners of inspiration, rearrange furniture, declutter closets, wash windows, add or adjust lighting, even make your own inspirational artwork with colors, images, or words that make you feel good in your space. This isn't about finding joy outside yourself but about bringing that purpose and vision from within to create environments that mirror who you truly are so that you can look around your space and marvel in your own awesomeness, every single day.

Revisit as You Evolve

It's natural and healthy for your purpose and vision to change as you move along in your journey. Continually revisit these exercises as you outgrow them and do so with a mindset of gratitude. Be grateful for what a purpose statement and vision board gave you at the time. Be grateful for how they helped you to grow and learn more about who you are and what you are truly capable of. Let it go with love, then create anew.

> CEO of Your Life Coaching Tip:
>
> Real progress happens when you are clear on what you're working toward. Having a life purpose statement and vision of what you want to create empowers you to make choices that propel you in the direction you want to go.

Cultivate a Heart of Peace

Recognizing My Own Heart of War

The Arbinger Institute is a coaching, training, and consulting institution that has been helping people shift their mindsets since 1979. Their book, *The Anatomy of Peace*, describes what it means to come from a heart of peace versus a heart of war and has been a powerful influence on how I understand the ways we can show up *for* ourselves and others, versus *against* ourselves and others (Arbinger 2015).

When you have a heart of peace, you see others as unique, valuable, and deeply human and approach them in this way. You show up with curiosity and compassion, understanding that others have an inner experience you know nothing about and treating them as though they too are coming from a heart of peace, open to co-creating solutions, and with value to contribute. With a heart of peace, it doesn't matter if the other person rises to the occasion with you (that said, someone is more likely to respond from peace when met with it). What matters is that you've done your best to show up in a way that respects the humanity of yourself and those around you.

When I first read the book, I was shocked by how much of myself I saw in the heart of war approach. When you have a heart of war, you approach others as objects. Reading that definition, I thought, "That can't be me. I would never treat a person as an object."

But then I read on.

The book describes how we can end up treating someone as an object when we go into self-preservation mode. When we unconsciously revert to protecting ourselves from pain, shame, fear, and so on, we unknowingly shift into a heart of war. When our Saboteurs tell us we're better than someone else or more deserving, that is a heart of war. But a heart of war is also our Saboteurs telling us *we're not good enough*.

When you feel unworthy, like you aren't measuring up or need others to see you a certain way, you are expressing a deep need to protect yourself. A heart of peace is open and curious. We simply cannot be open and curious when we're locked in a defensive state.

That I could be showing up with a heart of war was a jagged pill to swallow. But I quickly recognized times when I'd felt attacked and my defenses had shot up. Especially when the pandemic began and everyone was anxious, afraid, and unsettled. As I tried to cope with the ongoing crisis, I would find myself feeling annoyed, overwhelmed, afraid, or tired. I would coach all day, do my best to give time to my family in the evenings, and need time to recharge so that I had energy for my family and clients. With everyone needing more support, I was exerting more energy, and it was my friends who got the short end of the stick.

When a friend would call, I would get annoyed. Didn't they know how busy I was? I tried scheduling calls with friends like I scheduled clients but would still get annoyed that I had to spend more of my precious energy to keep those appointments. When I did speak with friends, I found myself treating them like clients, asking them questions and truly listening but never sharing anything about my own experience. I was stuck in "coach mode" when I needed to be in "friend mode." I needed to lean on people and let them support me, but with so little energy to spare, I didn't even realize how in over my head I was.

Recognizing that I had shifted into a heart of war was difficult but empowering. In recognizing those patterns, I also recognized that they are rooted in normal human instincts. As a human, like all humans, I am both worthy of my own forgiveness and strong enough to offer forgiveness and love to others.

Recognizing it empowered me to make the shift back to a heart of peace.

Connecting With Your Heart of Peace

From childhood, we are taught certain rules and ways of being that can contradict what our bodies and intuition tell us. In order to follow the rules and "be good," we learn to disconnect from the messages of our hearts in favor of security and acceptance. In adulthood, this is when we can get caught in a self-preservative mindset that closes us off to peace.

Following expectations as children can serve us well as we grow toward adulthood. But once we are on our own, life doesn't have those same clear paths and milestones. We're expected to find our own way.

Without strong inner leadership, it's understandable that so many of us struggle to move forward and become stuck in unfulfilling situations, patterns, and mindsets; that we can be showing up from hearts of war without even realizing it.

In times of chaos—whether it's a pandemic, election, global crisis, personal crisis, or even just the chaos of daily life—much of the stress and anxiety we feel is fueled by disconnection. That disconnection can serve us well in some areas: we learn to fit in, stay out of trouble, or succeed academically. We are often rewarded with acceptance and praise. In this way, the disconnection becomes a comfort zone. We turn into it when challenges arise in order to feel safe and secure.

That's a pattern we need to break. To show up with hearts of peace, we need to train ourselves to instead lean into connection with our core selves, especially during unsettling times. There is no guidebook for much of life's challenges. How does one make decisions about family, work, community, and even day-to-day life while coping with so much uncertainty?

Accept to Connect with Your Heart at Peace

Being intentional about reconnecting with your heart to shift into peace doesn't make the chaos go away; it makes the chaos manageable.

Our brains can be excellent problem solvers but aren't very good at accepting what we can't control. We can easily get stuck fighting against things we cannot change. That's where the "heart brain" comes in.

The heart brain sends messages to the head brain about how the body feels and more. In fact, the neurons in the heart send far more information to our brain than the neurons in the brain send back! It's a two-way street . . . with busier traffic on one side.

The heart brain also releases oxytocin. Oxytocin is often called "the love hormone." It is tied to emotions such as gratitude, trust, and relaxation, as well as reducing anxiety and helping us control those knee-jerk stress reactions that show up when our hearts are at war. By producing oxytocin, your heart creates a sense of calm and trust. When there is no guidebook, your heart brain is your guide, helping you lead yourself from clarity and responding instead of reacting.

Our emotional state is connected to our hearts. We feel this physically and intuitively. Our hearts beat harder when we're stressed, faster when we're scared or excited, or slower and steadier when we're calm. Because of that connection and the heart's ability to calm strong emotions and shift us into peace, our hearts have important qualities in terms of self-leadership, such as:

- Greater discernment.
- Intuitive clarity.
- Deeper connection with yourself and others.
- Inspiration for emotions like love, care, compassion, appreciation.
- The ability to see potential in the face of challenges.
- Clarity into the boundaries that are right for you.

(Heartmath n.d.)

Your heart is the place of Oneness. It has no polarity, only insight. When that insight is integrated into your full human experience, you can make better decisions for yourself, lead yourself with confidence and clarity, and show up from a heart of peace. You're able to fully accept yourself and everyone around you, treating everyone as worthy, valuable, and capable of co-creation.

In many ways, the heart is the seat of acceptance. It's where we relax into what is and release the anxiety of defending ourselves and needing to always be in control. By connecting with our hearts, our heads can tap into that acceptance to clear away all that stress, giving us the clarity to see the true possibilities in front of us.

Connecting with your heart leads you to peace.

Strengthening your Heart Connection

Many people who practice mindfulness find that when they tune into their heart brain (as well as the other "brains" throughout the body) it has a deeply connective effect on their well-being. It empowers them to step into the wholeness of themselves and feel a sense of oneness with the world around them. You cannot be at war with your world when you are one with your world. Strengthening your heart connection builds the inner resilience needed to avoid that heart of war shift.

Remember that if you want something different, you must do something different. The keyword here is "DO." Reading this book is great, but it can only help you if you step into action. Commit to bringing mindfulness into your life to strengthen your heart connection.

When the brain says, "I can't," "This is too hard," or "There's no way," reassure yourself that your brain isn't your only messenger. When these thoughts come up, take that moment to connect to your inner leader and shadow. Put your hand on your heart and breathe deeply. Say to yourself, "I love all parts of myself. I am enough. I am the CEO of my life."

You may find a different affirmation works better for you. One I love is saying "I am" on the inhale and "my breath" on the exhale. "I am my breath." Consider setting a daily alarm to help you remember to practice.

Find something that feels grounding to you; something that allows you to observe your mind chatter without judging or ruminating. Remember that no matter where your limiting beliefs or patterns originated, you are the one continuing to give them life. Just as those beliefs and patterns took time for you to integrate, it will take time AND small, consistent, intentional actions to integrate new beliefs and patterns.

The connection we have with ourselves is foundational. From that, we can build healthy connections with others. Not only is your heart packed with neurons, it also generates its own energy field (as all living things do). Science isn't yet clear on exactly what this means for us, but as humans, we all know what it means to feel the "energy" of another person.

We resonate differently with people depending on our own energy and theirs. A heart of war gives off a very different energy from a heart of peace. We know we can't control anyone else's energy, but we can control our own. By connecting within, we shift our energy, not only shifting into a heart of peace in how we show up with others, but also shifting the way their energy impacts us.

In shifting your energy, intention matters. Think about how you have shown up with others in the past. Then visualize how you would *like* to show up.

It can help to think in terms of replacement behaviors and mindsets. For example, "I tend to get defensive in times of conflict. I would like to replace that behavior with curiosity." Then visualize exactly what that will look like: "When confronted, I will act with curiosity by asking the other person what this looks like to them, how they feel about the situation, what is being impacted for them and what changes they would like to see." You cannot control how they react, but you can control your own actions, and the energy you put into your connections with others.

Ideally, choose just one change to make at a time. It will take intention at first. Visualize the change you want to make at the start of each day. You may even set an alarm for yourself to take a moment to reconnect with that intention.

When we're disconnected, we see the world through hearts of war. Negative energy from others impacts us more strongly. Misery loves company. But, when we show up with peaceful, heart-led, connective energy, we're less likely to be impacted by negative energy. Our connection keeps us grounded and whole.

On the flip side, our new energy attracts the positive energy in others, drawing us to other connected souls but also potentially drawing out the connected energy in someone who is struggling, helping them feel less chaotic in a chaotic world.

Leading From a Heart of Peace

I believe that each one of us has the power to become leaders in our own way. Most importantly, we have the power to become leaders of ourselves. The leadership skills I help people develop in a professional sense can be applied to all areas of life—not just work—to create empowering connections. Think about the relationships in your life today and how you've been showing up in them. Is it from a heart of peace or war?

If it's from a heart of war, forgive yourself.

For me, that was my first step. I had to forgive myself for my basic humanity so that I could fully accept my humanity—shadow and all—then forgive and accept the same in others, especially when it feels hard. This is how I choose to lead myself and be a leader to those around me.

Allowing yourself to wallow in shame, guilt, or any other negative feeling will only feed a heart of war. Acknowledge the feelings as they come up. Accept them, then let them move on. You are human, and that is enough. Forgive yourself for every time you saw yourself as "less than," or even "better than." For every time you sought acceptance from someone else instead of your own wonderful self. For every time you let yourself be led by a heart of war.

Give yourself love. Go within. Connect with your heart of peace. And lead from it.

CEO of Your Life Coaching Tip:

A heart of war can mean you're on the offensive or defensive, triggered by self-preservation mode. A defensive heart isn't looking for a fight but desperately trying to avoid one and can't help but see everything and everyone around it as obstacles to overcome. Work within to connect with your heart and bring it into a state of peace. From a heart of peace comes infinite possibility.

Author Your Thoughts, Author Your Life

So many of the people I work with stress over anticipated—but not yet realized—outcomes. They worry about things like money, the sale or purchase of a house, or a disagreement with their boss or partner that could have negative consequences. It is rational to worry about the outcomes of big or potentially impactful experiences in our lives. The thing is, though, the thoughts we feed get bigger. It starts with one thought. That thought generates a feeling. That feeling generates more thoughts, which then generate more feelings, and before we know it, we're exhausted with worry over what might happen.

When I was starting out as an entrepreneur, I worried frequently about money. What if a client didn't pay me on time? What if I couldn't hold onto clients? What if I couldn't pay my bills on time? What if I couldn't support my son? A single "what if" snowballed into an entire state of being that had me constantly on edge and drained of energy. I was trapped in a cycle of anxious thoughts creating negative feelings, which in turn caused even more anxious thinking.

When we aren't living mindfully, this happens without our intention, meaning our state of being is created almost entirely by factors outside ourselves. If we take control of this loop through conscious, mindful practices, we can take control of our state of being.

How Your State of Being Comes to Be

Humans are an adaptive species.

As we grow, every new experience can become formative. Our first jobs, first relationships, first romantic experiences . . . we adapt into those experiences. And many of us do so without intention. Through everything we touch, see, hear, feel, taste, smell, and intuit, we are receiving knowledge. That knowledge becomes what we know the world to be.

We are especially tuned into repetition. What is repeated becomes knowledge. For example, if the first two or three bosses you ever have are dictatorial-style managers, your brain begins to "know" that managers are just out to exert power. You don't expect fairness, compassion, and humanity in your work life because you "know" that it isn't the way of the world.

However, understanding how this works empowers you to take control of the process, shifting your brain away from negative repetitions and creating empowering repetitions for yourself. The beauty of the world we live in today is that we do not have to fit in to thrive. It's within us to create what we want for ourselves, find our own tribes or chosen families, decide for ourselves what works for us, and both seek it out and create it.

The psychologist Donald Hebb famously described this process as, "Cells that fire together, wire together" (Calbet 2018). When thoughts and feelings repeat within us, neurons fire together to create our understanding.

When we intentionally develop new habits and practices—particularly around the thoughts we cultivate and how we notice and respond to the feelings in our bodies—we can weaken old "wirings" and help new ones come into being.

In a way, it's a lot like reprogramming ourselves. We can almost literally upgrade our lives by deleting old programming and downloading new, better programming that enables us to create deeply intentional lives.

What's critical is that you lean into repetition. Harness that to create what you want for yourself.

Six Steps to Reprogram Your Thoughts

Step One—Identify the currently running program.

"I can't do this." "This isn't possible." "This is too risky." "I don't deserve this." "What will people think?" "I'm letting people down." "I'm not made that way." Whatever it is, give the program a name. For example, the "Not Good Enough Program." You might have more than one running. Address them one at a time.

Step Two—Terminate the program.

Decide to consciously terminate and remove the program. Visualize it being completely and permanently destroyed. You can even write out the old program and burn it, saying, "I release you."

Step Three—Choose a new program to download.

Choose something like "I Am Worthy," "Everything is Possible," "I Can Do This," or "I Deserve to Do What Fuels Me." Something that resonates, inspires, and opens you up to new possibilities.

105

Step Four—Visualize the new program downloading into you.

Sense how good it feels as every cell of your body accepts the new program. Visualize the benefits it will bring you—feeling worthy, loved, respected for who you are, and valued for what you do.

Step Five—Disable your fail-safe.

That old program may try to resurface, especially if you run into challenges or difficult circumstances. Don't allow this internal fail-safe to activate. Address whatever fears may be coming up. Acknowledge, embrace, and face them, head on. Remember how you destroyed it. Tap into the energy of your new program to keep moving forward.

Step Six—Repeat the cycle.

Negative thoughts are sneaky. They start off as reasonable caution, a risk that doesn't feel right, or something not going the way you hoped. Before you know it, an invasive program is taking over and holding you back all over again. When that happens, repeat the above steps to reprogram your thoughts.

Create Your World by Creating Your Beliefs

It is an uncomfortable truth that many of our beliefs—what we "know" the world to be—come from outside ourselves. In the past, I often had thoughts like, "What am I thinking, starting my own business? I should be focusing on financial stability for my family." Some of that uncertainty was mine, but what came from *outside* myself was the idea that I don't know how to make good decisions. Every time my ideas were shut down—whether it was the idea that I was in love at age seven, or my interest in psychology—the message I got was that others knew what was best for me, and I didn't.

When our early teachings leave no allowances for individuality, they push us to disconnect from our intuition, passions, and strengths—the best parts of who we are.

When a thought comes into your mind that holds you back, ask yourself if this is something you truly believe, where this belief came from, if it's right for you or working against you, and if it feels light or heavy.

Bring yourself right up close to your beliefs and explore them from all sides to determine whether they fit into the life you want for yourself. Some of your programmed beliefs may be good ones that you ultimately agree with. But beliefs that aren't right for you will only ever drag you down and hold you back from being You. Let them go.

You always have a choice. There's a saying that I continually go back to: "Your reality is a reflection of your strongest beliefs." If I can choose my beliefs, I can choose my reality. And that is a powerful realization.

Repeating the Cycle with Mindfulness

While your new ways of thinking need repetition, you also must stay aware of those old thoughts and beliefs trying to creep back in. Mindfulness practices give you moments of full awareness, allowing you to build that into your daily life. Intentionally create your way of being and decide who you are, how you will show up, what you believe, and what you will and will not accept.

Mindfulness is your moment to decide for yourself that your world can be what you want it to be. Instead of giving your power to the limiting, intrusive thoughts that originate from outside yourself, you are putting the power back into your own hands, building positive inner connections that become your state of being.

Meditation is an incredibly powerful way to connect your brain with your heart and body. It's in meditation that you actively accept all parts of yourself, forgive yourself for the negative programs you've allowed to run, and accept that as part of your journey. You can preemptively forgive yourself for any stumbles you'll have as you forge ahead and envelop yourself in love, empowering your body, heart, and brain to co-create a state of being that is truly and beautifully You.

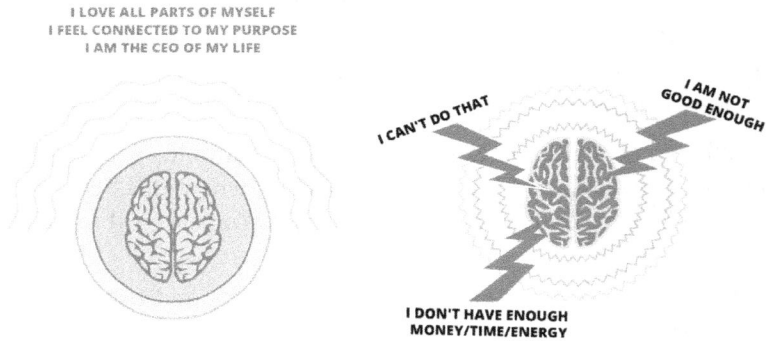

I LOVE ALL PARTS OF MYSELF
I FEEL CONNECTED TO MY PURPOSE
I AM THE CEO OF MY LIFE

I CAN'T DO THAT

I AM NOT GOOD ENOUGH

I DON'T HAVE ENOUGH MONEY/TIME/ENERGY

Graphic by Liz Lee, inspired by *Breaking the Habit of Being Yourself: How to Lose Your Mind and Create a New One* by Dr. Joe Dispenza

CEO of Your Life Coaching Tip:

Your state of being is yours to determine. Tap into habits and practices that put you, repetitively, into the CEO seat of your own life.

Set Healthy Boundaries

Imagine a CEO with a true open-door policy: people coming and going at all times, weighing in on every decision, giving directions, critiques, unsolicited feedback . . . they wouldn't be a very effective CEO. Everything important would fall to the wayside, and long-term goals would be impossible. The organization would be in shambles.

That imaginary CEO is one without boundaries. Boundaries are an important part of healthy relationships with others and ourselves. They keep us whole, empowering us to align with our own values and purpose while respecting the values and purpose in others. As the CEO of your life, you're not obligated to have an open-door policy. It's within your power (and often in your best interest) to simply close the door.

YES, the people around you will react. And YES, they might leave or withdraw whatever "carrot" they have for you. But if they do, ask yourself if these are the type of people you want in your life. Do you want to continue indulging people that don't love you as you are? Who don't respect what's important to you? Who can't value the purpose of healthy boundaries?

Of course, boundaries aren't easy, especially if others resist them. But living a life where you're constantly drained is a life of stress and stagnation. People-pleasing may seem easier, but only when aiming to please is your main priority. Once you look at your instincts objectively, you begin to see that the truly scary and uncomfortable place is the "comfort zone," devoid of boundaries, that leads you to give away pieces of yourself.

Boundaries Create a Better Normal

Boundaries are always important, but as I'm writing this book, the world is struggling with the Covid-19 pandemic. For many people, that has made boundaries more important than ever. Working from home has become more common, for those of us fortunate enough to have the option, and many clients have told me they need their own space—physical boundaries within their homes. I've seen everything from meetings in closets, to offices in bathrooms, to upended bed frames as room dividers.

These physical and visual boundaries are a great start, but they can be helped along by healthy *personal* boundaries. What's been truly inspiring is that as my clients recognize where they need to create personal boundaries in this "new normal," they're also realizing that these are boundaries they want to carry over into their post-pandemic lives.

Wherever you are in your life today, and whatever is going on around you, setting or modifying your boundaries may take you out of your comfort zone and your current normal. But, if you approach the process with intention, strengthened mind-body-spirit connections, and alignment with your leader within, those boundaries will help you create a better normal for yourself.

What Defines a Healthy Boundary?

"Boundaries are the distance at which I can love you and me simultaneously."

—Prentis Hemphill

When you feel safe and free within a space, that's when you know you have healthy personal boundaries. This is true in a physical space, but what I'm talking about are emotional, mental, and spiritual spaces.

Our personal "space" is connected to our inner well-being. When we feel that space is threatened, crowded, jumbled up, or otherwise not secure, that's an indicator that we don't have healthy boundaries in place. This can feel like doing everything to please others, fighting just to "stay afloat," feeling your life force is being sucked out, or just functioning in survival mode.

Think about a recent interaction you had with someone and ask yourself if you felt love for yourself and the other person in that moment. Use the word "love" not in a romantic sense, but a human one—that point at which you can fully love and accept yourself while fully acknowledging and respecting the other person.

Ask yourself, "Was I showing myself love? Did I feel securely aligned with my values and purpose? Did I feel safe showing up as myself with no protective armor or persona? Was I also seeing the human in the other person? Understanding that they had a whole inner experience I knew nothing about and accepting it without judgement or a need to change it?"

Many people are afraid to set boundaries that empower self-love. We're afraid of rejection or upsetting someone. Of love or affection being withdrawn. Of getting fired. Of being criticized, called selfish, or accused of being a bad employee, parent, spouse, friend, or child.

When you live your life afraid to set boundaries, just like the open-door CEO, people will walk in and fill your space with all their ideas, opinions, and demands, and it is hard to change. If that is where you're starting from, you are not alone. If you've set boundaries before but find they're no longer serving you and need to be adapted, you aren't alone in that either.

Get Comfortable with the Uncomfortable

If you truly want to end the draining, people-pleasing cycle, you must put up walls against situations and people that cause you to feel less than whole. In some cases, those walls will build stronger, more vibrant relationships with deeper connection through understanding. In other cases, those walls will be protective, keeping toxic people or situations at bay. Although it will not always be easy, remember that protecting yourself is not selfish! It's a vital form of self-care.

As a child, I had no voice of my own. Because I was not taught to say "no" when I was uncomfortable and always expected to respect adults unconditionally, I never developed self-confidence. Instead, I grew up believing that my thoughts and feelings were wrong and that it was up to authority figures to tell me what to think, feel, and do. Not having this confidence created many issues in my life.

In my romantic relationships, I had no experience advocating for myself. I had been taught to allow men to impose their expectations onto relationships without any pushback. I thought that was the way it was supposed to be; in my family, and the families around me, men set the tone, and women obeyed. I clearly remember a piece of advice I received just before my first marriage: "When your husband wants sex, you need to give it to him, or he will cheat on you." From this perspective, even my body was not truly my own, and if something bad happened in the marriage, it would be my fault for not doing what was expected of me.

Not speaking up for myself and not having any experience with setting boundaries led to many nights of pain and tears, wondering if it would ever end. The advice and beliefs I had been raised with stayed in the back of my mind for a long time, and it took so much work and energy to understand that my feelings were worthy and I had a right to express them.

There are many ways we can end up abused or taken advantage of when we aren't empowered to set our own boundaries—when we are taught that pleasing others matters more than respecting ourselves. As an adult, I learned that healthy boundaries aren't just about protecting ourselves from the bad but also about creating space for the good. As they guide us away from what isn't right for us, they guide us *toward* the relationships, opportunities, and pursuits that fuel us.

Setting boundaries is easier said than done, especially if the people around you are resistant and/or dealing with their own struggles. Remember to put your own oxygen mask on first. If you're holding others up without caring for yourself, you aren't being strong. You're being used. Eventually, you'll get used up—and that's when burnout sets in.

Ten Steps for Setting and Maintaining Healthy Boundaries

These ten tips and best practices will guide you to strengthen yourself within through holding up your boundaries:

One: Identify where you need to set or adapt boundaries.

If boundaries are the distance at which you can love yourself and the other person simultaneously, where is this missing for you? With whom do you not feel whole? Is there a relationship where you constantly feel the need to protect or prove yourself? Where you feel not good enough or that the give and take is out of balance?

Two: Accept the reality of the situation.

You may think, "If I just change this or that, if I just do a little more, if I just do this one thing . . ." Or you might think, "If *they* just change this or that . . ." In a healthy relationship—personal or professional—no one should have to compromise their values, overextend themselves, put up a false front, or employ any other inauthentic tactic to make things work. That isn't love, acceptance, or respect. Accept what is and what isn't.

Three: Let go of what they can't give you.

You could spend your whole life trying to get approval and acceptance from others and never get it. I depleted myself again and again to keep the peace or gain love. It only ever ended in me burning out. Whatever you fear losing—that person or their love—face it. Burn those limiting feelings if you need to. Just let it go.

Four: Prepare for resistance.

Change can be difficult. The person you're setting boundaries with may resist at first. Prepare yourself to handle this with compassion, confidence, and consistency in holding the boundaries you need. Toxic people will likely react negatively. Your boundaries prevent them from continuing as they want to. That is not your wound to heal.

Remember our definition of boundaries. No part of that says that the other person has to love you. That's not something you can control. Find the place where you can love yourself and see the humanity of the other person, then stand firm in that place. Where they choose to stand is outside your circle of control and responsibility.

Five: Remind yourself why you're doing this.

When someone reacts poorly to our boundaries, we're often tempted to revert to pre-boundary terms. Remind yourself of why you started this journey and that you cannot change others, only yourself. Talk it through with your support person. You need to stick with your new boundaries, and having people to support you is essential.

Six: Stay alert to red flags.

The person you're setting boundaries with might try to guilt trip you, call you selfish or inconsiderate, play themselves as victims, or gaslight you. They know how to make you feel guilty and how to break down your confidence. They will play on that to try to maintain the status quo. Be aware of these tactics, stay alert to them, and don't engage with them.

Seven: Be conscious of levels of awareness.

When you choose to be intentional about setting healthy boundaries, you're choosing to act from your highest level of awareness. The person you're setting boundaries with may be operating from a lower level. In showing up at a higher level, they may be inspired to bring themselves up as well. Or not. It isn't your responsibility, or within your power, to bring them up. Be open to their rising but stay firm in not getting pulled down. Always remember that if you *want* something different, you need to *do* something different.

Eight: If you are a parent, healthy boundaries matter twice as much.

Setting healthy boundaries with others sets a solid example for your children. Setting healthy boundaries with your children teaches them that boundaries are part, not a limit, of love. This means also respecting your child's boundaries. As parents, we can do this by aiming to be their guide, not their dictator. Let them explore, discover, and build a solid sense of self. Let them say no. Let them make choices. Show them that boundaries are meant to be respected in a loving relationship by respecting theirs.

Nine: Start small.

Some people are so eager for change that they start setting all their boundaries at once, and the situation becomes unmanageable. From my experience, both personally and in working with clients, I recommend setting (or adapting) one or two boundaries at a time. As those are established, gradually add more. Give the other person time to accept and adjust and yourself the time and clarity to be intentional in holding your boundaries respectfully.

Yes, it can be frustrating not to have it all done at once, but that is the cost of not having set them sooner. Moving forward, remember that this is why it's so important to have authentic conversations when situations arise. Doing so naturally builds healthy boundaries into the relationship so that there isn't a jarring burnout situation down the road.

Ten: Be mindful of your words.

The way you say things matters. Lashing out will inevitably get a negative reaction. Speak from a heart of peace, not a heart of war. Choose to see the humanity on the other side—a person with needs, wants, fears, desires, and struggles just like you. Get curious about what is going on with them. Even if you are "at war," you can show up with compassion. When you do so, others are more likely to treat you the same way, increasing the likelihood of peace.

Keep going back to that definition of boundaries as being able to love yourself and others simultaneously. Have compassion but don't capitulate. It can be hard when someone resists your boundaries, but holding firm is self-care. Here's what capitulation versus compassion might look like in practice:

Capitulation: "I'm so sorry. I didn't mean to upset you. Maybe we can find a compromise."

Compassion: "This is hard. I can see you're upset, and I get it. Change can be difficult. This boundary is important for me, and I need to stand firm."

Healthy boundaries—the ones we need in order to love ourselves fully—cannot be up for negotiation. Your happiness can't depend on anyone else's choices, just as someone else's happiness can't depend on yours. Compassion is acknowledging and accepting another person's discomfort, not taking responsibility for it.

It's hard, and many of us simply weren't raised to have confidence in our own inner experience. This isn't necessarily a failing of previous generations, but an evolution in our understanding of what children need to become healthy adults.

Be the person today that your child-self needed. This is how we create better lives for ourselves that ripple out into a better world. Choose to no longer settle for your comfort zones but to use boundaries as the building blocks of healthy emotional spaces for yourself. Create spaces that are genuinely comfortable and safe, allowing you to be yourself and grow yourself.

CEO of Your Life Coaching Tip:

To end the draining, people-pleasing cycle, you need healthy boundaries—a place where you can love yourself fully while honoring and respecting the other person. You have to put up walls against situations and people that cause you to feel less than whole. You are responsible for your wholeness and yours alone. Trust that others will find their own way if, and when, they're ready. And if you're a parent, remember that setting your own healthy boundaries and respecting your children's boundaries sets a loving example that will continue for generations.

Cultivate Healthy Relationships

Relationships form a significant part of your world. Like anything else, they have the power to fuel you or drain you, depending on how "safe" it is to be You within them.

While you cannot control how other people show up, respond, think, or feel, you can absolutely control your side of the equation. You can control how your energy is spent, how you show up and respond, how you deal with your own thoughts and feelings, and what you choose to accept from others.

There are many types of relationships, and I can't dig into them all in the span of one book. Instead, I've divided the guidance in this chapter into Personal Relationships, Dysfunctional and Abusive Relationships, and Professional Relationships.

Personal Relationships

Personal relationships include those we grew up with, as well as those we build for ourselves. For this section, I'm referring to close, intimate relationships such as immediate family, close friends, romantic partners, etc. For relationships that are more of the "friendly acquaintance" or "distant relative" variety, the guidance in the Professional Relationships section will help.

If you're fortunate, the people in your personal sphere are supportive of your growth. Ultimately, they want what is best for you and will support your journey to You.

But many of us are not so fortunate.

I felt so pressured by the expectations of my family and community that breaking free of the masks I'd cultivated was extremely difficult. I was afraid of what I might lose and how my relationships might change.

Leaning into the concept of the Hero's Story helped me put a new perspective on what I had experienced. One that allowed me to step out of the clouds and see my own story—past and future—with more clarity.

Remember that the goal of the Hero's Story is to put ourselves in the driver's seat moving forward. In childhood, choice was largely out of our hands. We weren't writing the book back then. Today, however, we can pick up the pen and start writing our next chapters and even—to some degree—rewriting parts of our past to create a story of empowerment.

Think about it this way: as far as today is concerned, what is your past? It's memories. It was all very real at the time, but today it is only memories; stories you tell yourself about who you are. Envisioning yourself as the Hero can help you reframe your story, take ownership of it, and begin to tell a different one; one that is no less true but leads to more joyful chapters ahead. This is not about taking the blame for things that were out of your control. It's about owning your story, your perspective, and what you make of where you are and how you choose to grow from here, including how you choose to show up in your relationships.

Bringing You Forward in Your Personal Relationships

Imagine writing the Hero's Story. You must work with what's already been written, but you have full say in how you shape the narrative moving forward. How can you write, from this point, in a way that positions you as the hero?

Who do you need to set boundaries with? Where and with whom do you need to speak your truth? Which relationships are fueling you, and which are draining you? How have you been showing up in those relationships so far? What choices can you make going forward to show up as You?

You may have relationships that are not what you want them to be. Accept the past, even if it wasn't what you would have wanted. Clarify how you can love yourself and the other person, simultaneously, and hold firm in that boundary.

Many of us compromise our needs, wants, and values or cultivate artificially "perfect" personas with our parents, siblings, or partners, thinking it will make the other person happy and safeguard the relationship. But you can't cut yourself into pieces like that. It isn't possible to feel truly loved and fulfilled when it doesn't feel safe to be your whole self.

In a healthy, harmonious relationship, you must be able to express your joy, anger, fear, limitations, desires, needs, satisfaction, jealousy, beliefs, disgust, fantasies, and every other facet of who you are. You must be able to share it all, without fear of judgment or abandonment. You must be able to ask, give, receive, and refuse and hold a safe space for the other person to do the same. The wholeness of You—your shadow and your light—deserves to be loved fully and completely. You deserve to feel nourished and safe and have the honor of creating that space for another person. Love is inherently vulnerable, and it's that vulnerability that creates connection and intimacy. Showing up as your whole self is one of the most vulnerable things you can do, and it's the path to the most authentic connection.

Most importantly, when you fully love and accept your whole self, that level of vulnerability becomes a lot less scary because you fully own your self-worth, and no one can take it away.

You Don't Complete Me . . . But You Do Teach Me

People don't complete each other. That's codependency, and it's a recipe for relationship burnout.

The nourishment and support we get (and give) in our relationships shouldn't be a crutch but more like fertilizer, giving us even more fuel as we build ourselves up, work towards our goals, face life's challenges, and create what we truly want for ourselves. Relationships require give and take, and there will be times when one person needs more than the other, but in the big picture, each person's needs and dreams are equally worthy.

What is beautiful in any relationship is what we can teach each other. We are all unique individuals with gifts to share. When we accept and love ourselves as whole beings, we're more open to what we can learn from those around us. In this way, every relationship can be a source of growth. When the relationship works out, you have two people continually supporting and encouraging each other toward becoming their best selves. If it doesn't work out, you are still a complete person, now with new experiences and lessons to continue your growth.

Compromise versus Sacrifice

For any two people to have a healthy, loving relationship, continual compromise must be part of the mix. How do you compromise in a relationship without cutting off pieces of your core self? At what point does compromise become sacrifice?

This is why self-awareness is so important. When you are connected to your inner leader and have welcomed your shadow with love and acceptance, you are able to intuitively feel when a compromise is right for you. Do certain things feel "light"? If they do, that's an indication that they are true for you. If they feel "heavy," you need to explore why.

When it comes to compromise, connect with your purpose and vision. Those are the parts of you that cannot be compromised. That's when compromise becomes sacrifice: when flexibility moves into martyrdom.

Usually, when a relationship begins to feel draining, it's because you've sacrificed instead of compromised. Whether you did so to meet the demands of the other person or of yourself, either way you were in control of the choice, and you are in control of making a different choice.

It's OK for Relationships to Be Hard

It's hard for some people to ask for help. It's hard for some people to receive help. It's hard for some people to say no. It's hard for some people to express themselves, and so on. These challenges are normal. In a healthy relationship, those difficulties come from inside ourselves and are opportunities for growth, which the right person will support. If those difficulties are driven or reinforced by the other person, that is not a healthy relationship.

We often hear that relationships are hard work, usually in the context of romantic relationships, but it can be true of all close relationships. That's healthy *if* the hard work fuels you, grows you, and brings out the best in you. It's also normal to hit rough patches, as long as you work through them together without sacrificing what truly matters to you.

Think about a current relationship.

Are you loving your whole self—the good, the bad, and the ugly?

What do you need to feel at peace, and is that realistic for you and for them?

Are you honoring the human in the other person?

Do you feel free to bring all parts of you forward?

Does this person show up as their whole self, trusting you to hold a safe space for them?

What do you want out of this relationship, and do you see it moving in that direction as it stands today?

What does being in this relationship truly mean to you?

Finally, what is the fear holding you back from expressing your truth in your relationship?

Whatever that fear may be, face the reality of it and address it, either by confronting it head on, journaling about it, burning it, getting some outside professional help, or all of the above. Do the inner work you need to do to embrace full self-acceptance.

Remember, whatever is happening in your relationships is a reflection of something happening inside of you. Relationships are our mirrors. If you feel the other person is not valuing you, ask if you are valuing yourself.

Relationships are there to help us grow. They are there to bring out what we need to heal. Go with that flow. Fighting against what is brought up is not healthy for you or the relationship.

If "the Worst" Happens

Let's say "the worst" happens, and this person no longer wants to be in your life once you start speaking your truth and being more you. Isn't that actually . . . "the best"?

You deserve to be loved for who you are, and that love needs to come from yourself first. It's hurtful when a relationship ends, but if you feel truly devastated by it, that's a sign that you need to work on giving yourself the love you deserve; that you've been looking outward for something you have the power to grow within.

Ask yourself, "What small step can I commit to today in order to start moving forward?"

That may sound like: "I commit to speaking my truth at least once daily where I previously didn't." Or, "I will start healing myself." Or, "I will have that conversation I've been avoiding. This is how I'll prepare for it, and I will have it done by X date."

When someone is unloving, that means they are not in touch with their true self. Don't take it personally and don't stoop to their level. When someone is acting from a heart of war, it's because they need love. It's a call for help (but not necessarily a call you are responsible for answering).

What's important to note is that I'm referring to someone *acting* from love and a heart of peace. Even when someone is not *in* love—the love of friendship, for example—they can act from a place of love. If, instead, they are behaving toward you in an unkind way, that is them allowing their wounds to drive them. That's their journey, not yours.

Your journey is to love yourself first. When you see all parts of yourself as worthy of love and acceptance, you *are* loved. It's as simple (and as complex) as that.

Decide for Yourself What Is Acceptable and What Is Not

These two questions will help you clarify what you want and what is acceptable to you.

- What do I really want in my relationship? What are my "must haves"?

Example: Truth, integrity, mutual respect, presence, healthy conversation, joie de vivre, personal growth, the ability to be me, trust.

- What is not acceptable? What are my deal breakers?

Example: Not impeccable in their word, not encouraging my personal growth, not emotionally available, subjugation, violence, emotional blackmail.

What you find unacceptable, you need to voice. You need to set boundaries. Be faithful to you. Don't look at the past or the future. How do you feel right now? What do you need to address now? Address those things. Don't hold resentment and don't withhold love. Speak your truth, forgive, and give and receive with love. When you do, miracles open up to you.

Take responsibility for yourself. Be firm with your boundaries and speak your truth. This is how you guide your story in the direction that's right for you. Do not compromise on what is unacceptable to you. That is sacrifice. Do not justify. Those are your needs, and they must be respected.

The Ties That Bind

Some relationships end. That's a fact of life. Whether you ended it, they ended it, or it was mutual, sometimes the energy of those relationships hangs around.

Do you have one of these relationships in your past? The one your mind keeps going back to, fantasizing over, reimagining, dwelling on? Maybe you feel like they were "the one that got away," or they hurt you and even though you've worked to heal that wound, you still ruminate on what they did?

Sometimes, even when we know it was right to end the relationship, we still feel something drawing us back to that person. I've come to see these as energetic ties or cords, keeping us tethered to another person.

Author Gabrielle Bernstein refers to these as "negative energetic attachments" that keep you weighed down by old relationships. She also has a unique and powerful method for cutting these ties in order to give yourself back that energy so you can channel it into better things for yourself. She has a great video on her website explaining this method and why it works: https://gabbybernstein.com/cut-the-cord/.

Here's how it works:

Find a comfortable spot to sit.

Straighten your spine, relax your shoulders, and unclench your jaw.

Roll out your shoulders, wiggle your jaw, gently turn your neck from side to side . . .

Begin breathing deeply and comfortably, allowing your breath to naturally lengthen as you breathe . . . in and out . . . in and out . . .

As thoughts come and go, simply notice them, then gently return to your breathing . . . in and out . . . in and out . . .

Invite the person into your mind's eye.

Notice the thoughts and feelings that come up . . . no judgment, just noticing.

Continue to notice your breath . . . in and out . . . as you experience the feelings.

Now visualize the energetic cord between the two of you.

Where do you feel the cord's connection to you? Your head? Heart? Stomach? Shoulders?

Visualize the cord and prepare yourself to release it.

Now visualize a sword of positive light in your dominant hand—it is a sword of peace.

When you're ready, take a breath in and on the exhale, lower your sword over the point of connection to cut the cord.

Inhale as you visualize the cord falling to the ground and exhale as you visualize it shrinking away into nothing.

Look back at the person without the connecting cord and release them, literally saying, "I release you, (name of person), to your own destiny."

Breathe in . . . breathe out.

Place your hand over the point on your body where the cord no longer connects and feel the wound healing.

Breathe in . . . breathe out . . . breathe in . . . breathe out . . .

Open your eyes whenever you're ready.

When you're done, you may feel ready to go about your day, you may want to sit with the feeling for a bit or journal about your experience.

Some people miss the cord and go back into their old patterns and the cord grows back. You might have to give it a strong *rip* and consciously say your goodbyes to it. It served its purpose for a time, and now it's time to move on.

Repeat the practice as many times as necessary, each time knowing that you are weakening the cord more and more while healing your wound more and more.

Dysfunctional and Abusive Relationships:
Your Relationship with YOU Comes First

It is not selfish to put yourself first. Self-love is where compromise, co-creation, empathy, forgiveness, vulnerability, courage, and a host of other relationship-strengthening elements come from.

Dysfunctional or abusive relationships are extremely difficult. Their toxicity can feel like a cloud of thick, poisonous smoke. They sap your energy and cloud your vision, leaving you feeling trapped. These dynamics make it nearly impossible for people under their cloud to be free. If you are truly going to be You, it is critical to identify any such relationships and get yourself out of that smoke.

How do you tell the difference between someone who's difficult or not a good fit for you and a truly damaging relationship? The world is full of difficult people and incompatible relationships where there isn't necessarily anything wrong; you just aren't a good fit for each other.

Someone who is abusive or no longer capable of having a functional relationship with you will try to convince you that you are the problem. They will make you doubt yourself and your leader within. Emotional or psychological abuse can be insidious and hard to pinpoint. Often, abusers will act like they're the only person with your best interests at heart—that they're the only person who truly cares for you—making it difficult to see the abuse for what it is. They say they love you. Or worse, that they *want* to love you, but *you* are making it difficult.

Abusers are often masters of manipulation, changing their personality according to whatever brings the attention they seek and makes them look good in the eyes of the public. It is important to remember that abuse is not always, or exclusively, physical. Emotional abuse or manipulation can take the form of:

- Transferring fault—they do something wrong and turn it around to be your fault.
- Gaslighting—making you doubt or question your perception of reality.
- Verbal abuse—belittling, criticizing, shaming, or other verbal bullying.
- Conditional withholding—of love, money, intimacy, safety, communication, or affection in order to coerce.
- Emotional blackmail—guilt trips, threats, or intimidation.
- Competition—constantly "one-upping" you or comparing and pitting you against others.
- Invasions of privacy—going through your things, ignoring boundaries, stalking or following, and denying physical or digital privacy.
- Dog-whistling—public comments that seem neutral to others but are known to be offensive, critical, or shameful to their target.

These are just a few of the tactics an abuser may engage in. They may even use only one.

Take an honest look at the list of behaviors above. Have you been subjected to any of these behaviors by someone in your life today or in the past? I experienced them all, although I didn't realize it until the past few years of my life. The damage and pain caused by emotional abuse is often so underhanded that even the victim is unaware.

One defining element of emotional abuse is that it's consistent behavior which, over time, breaks down your self-worth, making you feel that you need your abuser, that you are not capable of functioning on your own, that you are the "bad" one. In a relationship like this, whether with a boss, family member, friend, medical professional, or romantic partner, you can never be You. Abusers always put the onus of change on the other person, rather than themselves. They will never allow you to pursue what you truly want because that does not fit their needs.

*Please note that the following steps are aimed at dysfunctional or emotionally abusive relationships. If you feel physically unsafe or think you may be harmed by a partner, family member, or friend, please reach out to the National Domestic Violence Hotline (USA) at 1-800-799-7233. If you are in Canada, visit https://www.canada.ca/en/public-health/services/health-promotion/stop-family-violence/services.html for province-specific numbers and resources.

Five Steps for Handling an Abusive or Irreparable Relationship

Step One—Recognize it.
You need to recognize the behavior for what it truly is: abuse. Abuse can come from a place of hurt. Abusers may have their own psychological struggles or have learned their abusive behaviors from being abused themselves. This does not make them monsters or villains, but they are not your responsibility. If they are causing you distress and holding you back from being You, their impact on you is abusive, and you do not have to accept it.

Step Two—Get help.
Seek outside help to support you in rebuilding your self-esteem, accepting the relationship for what it is, and setting boundaries. It may be best to get support from someone who has been through an abusive relationship themselves because the experience can be difficult to truly understand if you have not been a victim of it.

Step Three—Accept the relationship for what it is.
Your abuser may be someone you wish you could have a loving relationship with. They could be a parent, sibling, or someone else truly meaningful to you. What's important is recognizing that the relation-

ship is what it is, and you cannot change it. Letting go of the relationship you wish for can be difficult and painful, and you may need time to grieve. Remember, you cannot change the relationship. You can only change the way you respond to it.

Your support person or group can help you become aware of the abuse and the impact it is having on you. Since they are not directly part of your abuse, they can see it more clearly. Often, victims are so poisoned by this toxic cloud that they do not realize the extent of the abuse and its impact. They typically downplay it, thinking there is something wrong with them.

Step Four—Set boundaries.

Take a step back and determine what boundaries you need to set in order to live the life you deserve; a life that feels good for you.

Healthy boundaries disrupt emotionally abusive dynamics. Expect the person to react negatively. Abusers don't like boundaries and may enjoy the challenge of them. They may try to convince you that you are harming yourself with your boundaries. Or they may make you feel guilty for setting them, saying things like, "How can you be so inconsiderate? You're hurting me. You're so selfish."

Regardless of how they react, do not go back on the boundaries you know are good for you. Remember that boundaries are not selfish. They are self-respect.

Step Five—Choose an approach.

With dysfunctional relationships and emotional abuse, you have two options: Gray Rock or No Contact.

The Gray Rock approach is for toxic relationships you cannot cut out completely. Maybe you share custody of a child, or maybe the abuser is a co-worker, neighbor, or someone you see at family events and cannot cut out without losing people who matter to you (Lancer 2019).

In this case, be a boring gray rock.

A rock shows no emotion, keeps answers short, and never provides justifications or explanations. Whatever they say, you can simply answer "Yes," "No," "Hm," or some other short, non-committal response, devoid of meaning, emotion, or opinion. Your reactions—especially arguments or justifications—are exactly what the other person is looking for. They're baiting you. Don't take the bait. Keep it businesslike. You are a strong and capable CEO of You. You call the shots in your life. When they can't get what they want and see they have no impact on you, they will go elsewhere to fuel their need for control and drama.

The No Contact approach is self-explanatory. When you realize a person is truly emotionally abusive, you may choose to end the relationship. You will never be able to reach your true potential within that environment. Why keep playing small to make others happy? If you try to discuss it with them and they refuse to understand or if they continually sap your energy and are toxic or manipulative, choose to end it. The more conversations you have, the more they will try to manipulate you, make you seem like the crazy one, and make you feel inadequate without them.

Cut them out completely. Remove them from your contacts and block their calls, texts, and social media profiles. If you need to, change your locks. Get a new number. Remove the poisonous smoke and don't let it back in.

Set a deadline for yourself to ensure you take action. Where emotional abuse is concerned, the sooner the better. You do not owe them any explanation or justification. Do not rise to their bait. Even their tears. Make the cut and move on. You can only start to breathe fresh air once you are out of that toxic smoke.

Stay strong. Stay the course. This is part of your survival and necessary for you to thrive.

Once you cut out an emotionally abusive relationship, the clarity of distance will lead to many realizations about the life you were living. These are healing. Let them in. Understand where they are coming from. Remember that it's impossible to always have approval from someone else. Seek approval from yourself first. That's the only approval that truly matters. Understand yourself. Become yourself. Celebrate yourself.

Professional Relationships

Many people have a "work self" and a "home self." But upholding a persona is draining. It isn't just the energy you put into it, it's also the energy that gets crushed by the weight of expectations. This can leave you feeling stuck, unfulfilled, drained, overwhelmed, and burnt out, and those feelings don't stop at work. They carry over into other areas of your life.

People will often say things to me like, "I have to be professional," "There are certain expectations at my work," or the ever-popular "I want to keep my work life and personal life separate." These are valid concerns that *do not* mean you have to break yourself into pieces in *any* area of life.

Here's the truth: You only have ONE self. We can't compartmentalize ourselves into different categories. When we try, it backfires, but it backfires so gradually that we aren't always aware of what's happening. The result of that slow burn? Misery. Exhaustion. Sickness. Conflict. Stress. An internal struggle that eats you up, leaving your soul yearning for something else.

Dropping the work persona allows you to connect with others in healthier ways, without sacrificing professionalism. Connections that honor the human in both of you. You also free up your energy to create, inspire, and lead, if not in a leadership role, then leading by example and by the energy and intention you bring.

The most joyful, productive, and engaging workplaces embrace the mantra that "weird is welcome." Nothing about any of us is truly weird. But the idea of bringing our whole selves to work really does feel uncomfortable for many of us. It's time to put an end to that, so we can thrive in our wholeness in all areas of life.

But let's face it. Not everyone has the privilege of working for a company that recognizes this. So, if that's not your situation, how can you be You? How can you bring your whole self forward, break the people-pleasing cycle, stand in the knowledge that you are good enough and deserve respect, and lean into the unique value of yourself and others?

How do you bring out your unique contribution when the environment isn't set up for it?

Years ago, I was working in a struggling environment and felt strongly that we needed an energy shift. In my personal life, I'm passionate about "energy medicine" and what some people term "alternative practices." One of those is smudging—using sage to clear negative energies. There is, of course, more to it; it is a sacred practice, and if you are interested in how it's done, there is a more detailed account on my website, www.CEOofYour.Life.

I desperately wanted to smudge the office to clear out the stagnant and negative energies. But I had this whole professional persona that was separate from my home persona. I didn't have the confidence to bring "home me" into the office because I was worried what other people would think. So, I came in super early one morning to smudge when no one was around. Secret smudging!

Not as secret as I'd hoped, it turns out. I was "caught" by one of the company founders, who arrived early for an important meeting.

He gave me a strange look but went about his day. Later, he came up to me and told me how well his meeting had gone, and maybe it had something to do with my sage?

I was speechless and still uncertain about merging my work and home personas. But, as time went on, I noticed myself feeling lighter at work. People heard about this "other" side of me, and it mostly made our relationships feel more natural and at ease. A mask had come down, and we could be people with each other instead of personas.

I started letting my masks down more and more, allowing myself to be fully Me. I still maintained my professionalism, but I felt more complete and engaged in my work, and I truly felt that this had a positive effect on the people around me as well.

This is what I recommend to you:

Ask yourself what unique contribution or essence of yourself you would love to bring forward. Are you bringing that aspect of yourself forward currently? If so, great! Keep it up!

If not, ask yourself what is holding you back. Face your fears and limiting beliefs head on so they have no power over you and no longer hold you back from bringing your best self to the work that you do. Ask what concrete steps need to be taken for you to bring this part of yourself forward. Do you need to speak with a manager or HR representative? A coach, therapist, or healer? Or is it a matter of setting the intention to do something of your own, every day? Maybe share an idea you would normally hold back, proactively ask for feedback, recognize a coworker's efforts, spend twenty minutes a day on a side project, or request a meeting with your manager to talk about your goals or what you want to bring forward. Start a vision board, do a walking meditation at lunch . . . take yourself outside your comfort zone in a way that is aligned with your values and strengths. Give yourself a timeline and stick to it. Perhaps have an accountability partner to support you.

Whatever you're stifling under a persona, whether at work or in another area, it will drain your happiness.

Your Perfect Work Environment

You, and only you, must take responsibility for your life, including your professional experience. Ask yourself, "Have I been showing up from a heart of peace or war?"

When you show up with a heart of peace, you see everyone as deeply human, with their own experiences, perspectives, and challenges, opening yourself up to a co-creative approach of progress, creativity, and collaboration.

On the other hand, if you show up with a heart of war, your thoughts, behaviors, and choices may be driven by judgement, anger, defensiveness, bitterness, justification, depression, hurt, irritation, etc., making your professional relationships truly draining.

If you go into situations or conversations already playing out arguments in your head—feeling like you need to win, put someone in their place, show them how they're wrong, or turn them to your way of thinking—those are classic "war" mindsets, and you're already closed to the possibility of working together.

The first step is You. If you are not happy with your environment, first consider how you're showing up, then get clear on what you DO want. When you lack that vision, you get stuck—either in one place or a cycle of unfulfilling role after unfulfilling role.

A vision board helps focus your thoughts and energies on what you want to create. So, yes, it's arts and crafts time!

Your "Perfect Work Environment" vision board should include all elements of what that looks like to you:

What is your ideal job?

What is your role?

What impact do you have?

How do you feel going to work every day?

What type of environment are you in?

What energies/personalities do your leaders/coworkers/employees have?

What does a typical day or week look like?

What type of salary and benefits do you have?

Is any training needed? If so, what would it involve?

Find images, quotes, and affirmations to create your vision board and concentrate your energies and actions toward making it happen. Your thoughts create your reality by driving your choices and actions. They will do that whether you put yourself in control or not. Visualize what you want and take intentional steps toward it.

Don't stress if you aren't sure of all the steps at first. Most people aren't. Focus on the first step, then the next, and so on. Consistently reference your vision board to ensure those steps are aligned with what you want to create. Course correct as needed.

What About Jerks?

I can just imagine some of you thinking, "But what if my boss/employees/co-workers are just jerks? What if they don't respect me? How do I create healthy work relationships if the people around me are the problem?"

Remember, everything starts with you. There's a great line from the TV show, *Justified*: "If you run into an asshole in the morning, you ran into an asshole. If you run into assholes all day, you're the asshole."

Now, I'm not calling you an asshole. But maybe you're being one . . . to yourself?

If you don't respect yourself and your boundaries, neither will others. When you truly respect and accept yourself, the respect and acceptance of others has less power to derail you.

Set clear limits, even with your boss. Review your job description if you feel you're being asked for more. If you're going beyond your job description, are those steps bringing you closer to what you want? Are they helping you achieve the goals you've set out, or are they putting you off track?

If extra work is derailing you, you may be surprised by how receptive leadership is to remedying that. Your success matters to the overall success of the company.

If the extra work is taking you closer to what you want, discuss that as well. Be open about what you want to work toward and ask about what career paths are possible within the organization. Don't wait for someone else to notice. Lead yourself. Be *your* CEO.

Until you face your feelings, you're fighting against them. Keep your goals in focus. Assess your strengths and do everything you can to bring your gifts forward, every day.

Leading From Within

There will always be external forces to deal with. When you choose to be the CEO of your life—to fully step into You—you must take full responsibility for *how you respond* to those forces. If you're struggling with professional relationships, lean into that responsibility. Be your own hero, not the victim of circumstance.

Leading from within may mean expanding your tool kit. That's a good thing because positive tools you use at work can usually also be integrated into your personal life. Two of the most impactful leadership tools I've learned came from the Coaches Training Institute: Third Level Listening and powerful questions. Here's how they work:

Third Level Listening is about full observation and mirroring back. Observe how people respond: their body language, the intonation of their voice, their energy level, the direction of their gaze. Observe it, then mirror it back, openly and without judgement: "I feel like you're low on energy today. How are you?" Or "You seem excited about this project. Tell me about it." It's a strong skill that creates connection and helps people be themselves.

Powerful questions involves asking open-ended questions, especially in times of conflict, that really get people thinking, like: "What is most important to you here? What does that look like to you? What's the end result you'd like to see?" Ask questions to get them thinking about what's going on for them and what they want to create. This empowers you to find common ground and collaborate more effectively.

A great deal of conflict can be overcome when we feel heard, seen and supported. You don't have to agree with someone to accept and respect their perspective. Hear what they're saying. Acknowledge their experience and knowledge. Provide honest (but respectful) feedback and speak your own truth, trusting that it will be met with the same respect and acceptance. If it isn't, you really haven't lost anything. When it is, you will gain so much.

It's about co-creating relationships of peace, and it starts with you.

CEO of Your Life Coaching Tip:

Every relationship has one element that you can fully control: You. In fact, it's the only element you fully control. If you have a relationship that is troubling you, or that you want to take to the next level, turn your perspective back onto yourself. How can you author your next steps in a way that you are your own hero, advocating for yourself and owning your self-worth?

Part III

Bringing You Forward to
Create Your World

Embracing Confrontation

Whether at work or in life, people want more from their conversations than they are getting. Something I hear frequently from clients is that they find themselves leaving conversations without having said what they really wanted to say, getting the answers they needed to move forward, or getting commitments to put things into action. This is a struggle I know well—not just because a huge part of coaching focuses on having better conversations, but because I lived with that struggle for years.

Why do so many of us struggle to get anything meaningful out of conversations? Because we are afraid. We fear the other person's response, fear rejection or our ideas not being important, or fear the other person's position and how they might handle the information.

We're afraid of confrontation. And fear is a powerful feeling.

Fear of confrontation is common, but it isn't sustainable. When you hold back your opinion, when you don't ask the questions you need to ask, when you avoid important topics, how is that serving you?

Confrontation is Not the Enemy

In the past, I ran from confrontation. Every time I did, I shoved more of myself into my shadow.

Only with my current partner did I begin to feel comfortable with confrontation. I vividly remember the first time I truly understood how much I had changed. It was about a year into our relationship. At that point in my journey, I still did not have full acceptance of myself: I was stuck in a stage of, "What will he think? What will he say? How will he react?" My head would be spinning, and I would get tongue-tied. At the time, I believed I had good reasons to hold back. After all, I wanted the relationship to work! Surely, censoring myself was the right move?

We were on a road trip. I *love* road trips. Like taking a walk or doing the dishes together, there's something about being side by side instead of face-to-face that allows conversation to flow with ease. Even with that ease, I was still holding back. I wanted to know—needed to know—if he had long term intentions for our relationship. I needed to know if we were on the same page.

Finally, he spoke up. "I can see you're holding something inside."

I hesitated.

If I voiced my thoughts, what would happen next?

He continued. "If we can't be real, what's the point?"

Oh, I was nervous. I asked myself what I was so afraid of. What was the worst that could happen? The worst that could happen was that he wouldn't feel the same way. It would hurt, but I would have answers, and I would be able to make my next decisions with clarity. Truthfully, I was afraid of having to make those decisions.

I took a deep breath. "We have been dating for a while, and it has been great. I do believe in living in the moment and enjoying one day at a time. But, at the same time, I would like to know if you see yourself staying with me for a longer period of time—seeing as you mentioned, at one point, getting a job in another country."

There. I had said it. Decision made and followed through. How he chose to respond was now in his hands.

He replied. "This has been my longest relationship to date. I am here with you because I want to be here with you, and when I think about my future, I can't imagine anyone else I would rather be doing this with."

I couldn't believe my ears. I smiled and felt a wave of relief wash over my body. I felt I was in the right place, on a highway in the middle of nowhere, looking at the moon and the stars, with the right person. From that point on, every time I felt a difficult conversation coming up, I would remember his words: "If we can't be real, what is the point?"

He was right. I believe we are born to live our truth. That will inevitably mean confrontation, and I needed to embrace that aspect of being Me.

As I started practicing confrontation, I noticed something beautiful. Those conversations brought me closer to myself and others. They served as building blocks to healthier relationships and stepping stones to better outcomes. It taught me a powerful truth: Confrontation is not the enemy. Avoidance of confrontation is.

Successful people recognize confrontation as the path of progress and choose to embrace it as a partner in their journey. This mindset empowers them to clear up misunderstandings, strengthen bonds, and lead themselves and others from a heart of peace. One conversation at a time, you can alter your world by altering how you approach it. However, when you avoid confrontation, you allow people and circumstances outside yourself to direct your journey.

Don't let fear push you off track. Recognize that healthy confrontation is simply a tool to help you build what you want for yourself.

Recognizing and Implementing Healthy Confrontation

Healthy, successful confrontation is an act of peace and collaboration. Rather than an approach of blame, shame, and judgement, it requires an approach of curiosity. Approaching confrontation with a war-mindset is combative and accusatory: "You're always disagreeing with me! It's like you don't even want to make this work." Approaching from a peace-mindset seeks common ground: "I notice we often have trouble agreeing. I'd like us to work together on this and create some solutions. What has your experience been?"

It's a simple example, but you can see how the approach of curiosity opens possibilities while the other approach pretty much shuts the door on possibility.

When you've held back for so long, though, where do you even start? How do you actually embrace confrontation and have the difficult conversations that need to be had?

There are three steps for implementing healthy confrontation:

Step One—Turn the finger around.

Is there something you need to work on or improve? Is there something you believe you are doing (or have done in the past) that is contributing to the problem? Own your part and take responsibility, without playing the victim. Keep in mind the expression, "If you never heal from what hurt you, you'll bleed on people who didn't cut you."

Psychologist, anthropologist, and author Dr. Alberto Villoldo tells us, "Own the parts of yourself that make you feel uncomfortable, and no longer hold anyone else responsible for your pain or happiness." When you own your part, you own your happiness.

Step Two—Get clear on who you're dealing with.

I really appreciate the advice from Dr. Henry Cloud in his book,

Necessary Endings (2011). He says there are three types of people: the wise, the foolish, and the evil.

I call them the Proactive, the Status Quo, and the Toxic.

A proactive person is ready for progress and will likely be receptive to a conversation. A status quo person is afraid of change and may shut down in the face of confrontation. A toxic person is . . . toxic. Confrontation of any kind is unlikely to be productive with them.

When it comes to someone you believe to be proactive or status quo, aim for courage and compassion. Remember that they are human, and even the most proactive person may struggle with confrontation. They will experience emotions, and you may witness those emotions. That's OK. As long as you are both committed to curiosity and understanding, you'll be glad you had the conversation.

If you're dealing with a status quo person, they are likely afraid to make changes. If they continue to dig their heels in or avoid acknowledging the problem and/or your feelings, you need to set limits and consequences.

Here are some examples of setting limits and consequences with a status quo person:

"I love you and want us to be closer, but for that to happen, I need my feelings and opinions to be respected. I would like to try counseling together. If you're open to it, I will set up the appointment. If not, I feel the relationship has gone as far as it can, and I will have to end it."

"Your argumentative behavior is taking a toll on the team. I've offered solutions, and I do not feel you are open to change. In tomorrow's meeting, I would like to see cooperation, support, and constructive input from everyone. If that's not something you can contribute, we will need to take some HR measures. We all want this project to go smoothly. I would be happy to help you out if you are open to it."

"I understand the challenges you've had lately. Feeling stressed and anxious is reasonable. However, I can't accept the way you've been speaking to me. I don't feel that my feelings are heard or respected when I bring them up. Our friendship matters to me, but my well-being matters too. I'd like us to give each other some space so we can both sort through our feelings. Let's give it a week and talk then."

A status quo person is often afraid of change, so think empathy but not doormat. Offer your help, if possible, but do not let their fear derail you. Set clear limits with consequences and follow through if your needs aren't met. How the other person responds to consequences is their responsibility, not yours. Remember, limits and consequences are not punishment for someone else. They are boundaries for YOU. Boundaries keep you connected to your core self and on the path that's right for You.

If you find yourself dealing with a toxic person, I recommend going no contact. If you need to get external enforcement from police or a lawyer, do it. There is no conversation that will change a toxic person's behavior. Instead, go straight to consequences. Speak firmly and clearly. Get to the bottom line while maintaining a heart of peace and compassion. Here are some examples:

"You have consistently hurt me. This relationship is over. I am leaving."

"Your behavior is unacceptable and is creating a hostile work environment. We have made the decision to place you on a performance improvement plan. A meeting has been set up with HR to go over what that means moving forward."

"Your words hurt, and you consistently refuse to acknowledge this. Do not attempt to contact me, as I will no longer respond."

Keep it short and simple, then FOLLOW THROUGH. If you waver, it will only encourage them.

In personal relationships, you may also choose to cut off contact with no explanation. This person has consistently and intentionally hurt you. You don't owe them any explanation or justification.

The Toxic Person You Cannot Cut Out

You may have a toxic person in your life that you cannot cut out.

In this case, choose the Grey Rock approach. Keep all communication business-like, void of emotion, and stick only to facts and basic information that must be shared. If possible, communicate only by text and/or email. Remember that *not* responding is a response. If you've said what's required of you, you can choose not to reply to any further attempts at engagement on their part. Do not embrace confrontation with this person.

For yourself, you may choose to:

Accept them as they are, realizing they will not change. Let that weight go.

Forgive them, not for their benefit, but to liberate yourself from the poison of resentment.

Wish them well (in your heart, not in person).

Some people have reported sending a toxic person love through their meditations and later noticing a shift in the other person. It's a possibility, but it is in no way your responsibility to initiate someone else's shift. What you might gain, however, is peace in your own heart.

There's a saying that, "Holding onto anger is like drinking poison and expecting the other person to die." Sending love is about releasing yourself from the poison of that toxic cloud.

CEO of Your Life Coaching Tip:

Embracing confrontation is essential to progress and well-being and keeps you firmly in the CEO seat of your life. Partner with confrontation, prepare yourself for who you are about to confront, and approach the conversation with peace and curiosity.

When Confrontation Isn't an Option

Whether you're struggling with a toxic relationship, dealing with old wounds caused by someone no longer living, or working through connections from the past you don't wish to renew—a former teacher, neighbor, or partner, for example—confrontation may not be an option. You may find yourself stuck in your head, spinning imaginary conversations, and never getting a sense of peace. In this case, healing is still possible even without establishing contact.

Healing Writing

Writing is a powerful healing tool. You don't have to be a "good" writer. This kind of writing is meant only for your own eyes and heart. Writing taps into the rational, analytical part of your brain, allowing the free thinking, intuitive part to roam free. When you write, with no plan other than to get your thoughts out, you release any mental blocks holding back your true emotions and intuition.

Confronting fears and problems head on, in the safe space of pen to paper, allows you to move through, and past, those challenging inner experiences. Writing clarifies your emotions and the bare facts, allows you to confront your feelings without confronting the person, and reduces the intensity of your emotions. Getting your feelings out on the page allows you to see the situation from a different perspective and uncover new ideas and possibilities as you come to better understand yourself, your motivations, and your wounds so you can begin to heal. Finally, writing helps to clarify the choices or paths in front of you so you can decide which aligns best with what you want to create.

Journaling is one of the most common forms of healing writing. I strongly recommend trying it. Journaling about stressful events, relationships, or circumstances can help you feel heard, which can reduce the impact of these stressors on your physical and mental health.

Even though a journal is meant for your eyes only, it can still feel scary or uncomfortable to unleash your emotions, not knowing what you might uncover. Take a deep breath and remember that you can do this at your own pace. Imagine yourself as an archaeologist, carefully brushing away the debris, layer by layer, pausing at times to just sit with what's emerging, excavating small sections at a time. This is your journey. You set the pace.

One technique is to start by writing down the dominant emotion you're experiencing—just the word. Then go from there. You've named the emotion. Now what? What else is coming up for you? Write in any way that feels good—paragraphs, point form, words clouds, drawings—it's for you and you alone.

Another form of healing writing is to compose a letter with no intention of sending it. A healing letter gives you a safe space to freely say what you need to say so you can start to heal and move on. It's a space to drop your masks without fear. To just be You, shadow and all.

Preparing to Write

Before writing a letter or journal entry, take a moment to remember that you are enough, exactly as you are. Whatever you write will not be good or bad, right or wrong, but simply a reflection of your inner experience. The things you may hesitate to put down are often the things that most need to get out. Embrace all of it.

Below is a condensed version of a healing letter I once wrote. For me, this took a lot of courage, but it helped me work through some difficult things that were creating roadblocks for me:

"Namaste,

It's been two years since I've seen you. Mostly, this distance feels good. Healthy. I can see more clearly what I believe versus what you wanted me to believe. I am happier and more confident, and my relationships with my partner and son have improved incredibly. I have created my feeling of family.

I would have liked you to be a part of it, but I felt you could never accept who I truly am. I couldn't even tell you about my relationship because I knew I would be scolded, judged, and reminded of past mistakes.

To the outside world you are charismatic and smart. I always admired that about you. Yet, with people close to you, you are another person. Unless someone sees things the way you do, you are not happy.

I feel you never saw me as an individual with my own unique gifts. You just wanted me to have good corporate jobs, get married, and do things 'the right way.'

That's not me. I've made mistakes, but I also grew up never feeling loved for who I truly was. I lacked confidence and accepted what I thought I was worth.

Every day it's a choice not to be in touch with you, and it's not an easy one. It hurts. I do wish things could be different. We never saw eye to eye, and I am tired of being put down, hurt, and not feeling comfortable or respected for being me.

I will never be who you wanted and am done trying.

Guilt comes in because I know in your mind, you did your best. And then I ask myself, 'is it my intention to hurt you?' The answer is, 'of course not,' so then I rationalize that I really have no reason to feel guilty.

My relationship with you helped me create who I am and inspire others to take steps toward who they really want to be. For that, I'm grateful.

I will always hold a place in my heart for you. I do love you and am grateful for everything you did to help me consciously and unconsciously be who I am today.

In Munay, Melissa."

After writing my letter, I decided to share it with my healer, the late Sanjay Nimar. He asked powerful and compassionate follow-up questions, which helped me dig even deeper and heal even further. He guided and supported me in so many ways, and I will forever feel a deep connection with his beautiful spirit.

You may choose to share a letter or journal with someone you trust, or you may choose to keep them to yourself or even burn your writings in a healing fire ceremony. Whatever feels right to you.

Release to Move Forward

When confrontation isn't an option, you still need a healing outlet. Emotions are complex. Thoughts and feelings can race around in your mind, bumping into other relationships and areas of your life. Writing is simply a tool to calm those emotions so they stop knocking into everything.

Thich Nhat Hanh wrote, "When another person makes you suffer, it is because he suffers deeply within himself, and his suffering is spilling over." If you continue to suffer and be complicit in your own disempowerment, you're not just hurting yourself. That suffering will spill over into the relationships that are truly meaningful and positive in your life.

CEO of Your Life Coaching Tip:

Pour your heart out through a pen. Speak from where and when the hurt happened. Writing will help you release unhealthy emotions and unexpressed words and let go of what could have/should have been. If you feel you need more help processing your emotions and healing your wounds, talk with a coach, healer, or therapist you trust.

Shifting Your Energy

Our thoughts, beliefs and actions are the input that create our worlds. If the input is always the same, how can we expect the output to ever change? How can we create anything new if we keep working with the same materials?

The Momentum Tunnel

Your past is made up of patterns, assumptions, beliefs, and comfort zones you established or absorbed throughout your lifetime. All this input carries momentum. It drives your future, determining how your story plays out, unless you stop to examine it.

Look back at past relationships, career moves, friendships, financial decisions, health and wellness incidents, periods of uncertainty, interests you picked up and/or abandoned. You can begin to see how all those events and patterns created your experience of life. Sitting in the present, you can probably also see how the stories you tell yourself about your past have been driving what happens next. Your story has been unfolding with its own momentum.

When you start to examine and retell the stories, it shifts the momentum, taking you out of a tunnel that is no longer serving you and empowering you to create a new tunnel for yourself. Your current momentum tunnel already has your future determined—if you allow the force to continue. If your current patterns remain unchanged, they will repeat. It's what patterns do. To shift your tunnel, it helps to understand that momentum is energy.

Energy, as I've come to know it, is the fourth element of mind, body, and spirit. It's the force flowing through them, connecting them, and even connecting us with the people and environments around us. Our energy is so much of who we are, how we show up, and the impact we have. It's our momentum tunnel at work.

As children, we don't choose the energy around us. Much of how we perceive the world, and how our momentum tunnels are mapped, is influenced by the energy of our environment. This is a big part of how generational cycles are created, as we guide each new generation—consciously or unconsciously—onto similar paths with similar patterns. Yes, it's hard to change something so deeply ingrained in ourselves and our culture, but remember that *all* energy creates momentum, which means you can create it in a new direction.

What, exactly, is this energy? In his book, *Breaking the Habit of Being Yourself,* Dr. Joe Dispenza writes that at an atomic level, humans are only 0.00001% matter (2013). The other 99.99999% is energy. You, like me, are probably not an astrophysicist, and this may sound a little strange. Astrophysicist Ethan Siegel published a great article in *Forbes* titled "You Are Not Mostly Empty Space" that explains this in a new way that's a little more accessible to us non-rocket scientists (Siegel 2020).

So, energy is . . . You. You are energy! It sounds unbelievable until you experience an energy shift for yourself—noticing, and even intentionally generating, the full experience of an energy shift and the impact it has on your state of being. It's a moment of, "Wow. That's me. I am that energy!"

Energy and Levels of Perception

I mentioned body, mind, spirit, and energy as four elements of the self, but they are also different levels of perception—how you perceive and, therefore, respond to everything around and within you.

Here is what is perceived and understood at each level:

Energy—Pure knowledge, wisdom, connection to the Universe. When you simply know that you are OK, connected, and worthy, that is your energetic perception.

Spirit—Images, visualization, myth, ritual/ceremony. When you shift your emotions through a fire ceremony or connect with a loved one through a traditional practice, that is your spirit perception.

Mind—Words, feelings, senses, intuition. Your thoughts are your mind perception. This is where you work to make sense of the world around you.

Body—Cells, molecules, hormones, neurons. Your feelings are your body perception. It's your intuitive sense of what's going on in and around your physical body.

Each of these levels informs the next so that energy informs spirit, which informs mind, which informs body. This means that all levels— all of your full self—reflect the state of your energetic self. If you have distress at the energy level, it's natural that you would struggle at other levels as well. If you're often asking yourself things like, "Why do I keep doing that? Why do I keep making the same bad choices? Why do I keep attracting the same type of people or problems?", chances are the core issue is with your energetic self. It is riding the momentum of deeply ingrained patterns, assumptions, and beliefs that are simply not working for you. Even if you aren't tuned into your energetic self, it absolutely is still driving you; your spirit, mind, and body are all reacting to what they're receiving from that self.

How Energy Can Shift

Meditation and mindfulness, continually connecting with the present, being intentional in how you show up and respond, setting healthy boundaries, and other genuine self-care practices are all intentional acts of tuning into your energetic self so that you can shift your energy—your input, your raw materials— and thereby shift your momentum tunnel.

All the exercises, activities, powerful questions, and tips in this book are designed to help shift your energy and create momentum in the direction you truly want to move toward. That said, these practices don't always work for everyone or every aspect of life. When you are struggling at the energetic level, you can develop blockages and inner defenses that keep you locked in your momentum tunnel.

This is why, whenever I'm working with a client experiencing a blockage, I suggest energy work.

Energy Work? Really?

I have always felt drawn to things that many people thought were pretty . . . out there. And I believe I'm drawn to these things for a reason. It's part of my purpose on this Earth. Before signing up to become a certified Master Energy Practitioner with The Four Winds Society, I hesitated, worried about what people might say. I was afraid of bringing this part of myself forward.

I coach a lot of leaders and corporate teams. I do this because I believe I can have a real impact. I know the business world: the pressures and needs and what's missing in many corporate cultures. How would my corporate clients react to a coach who's also an energy healer? Would they think I was less of a leadership coach? That I was too "woo-woo" for the business world?

But that was my Saboteurs talking. I knew that being on this journey meant stepping fully into myself, owning all parts of Me, and living them courageously. No more shoving parts of myself into my shadow. I signed up and did the work to get certified. It took guts to do it, and even more guts to put it on my website, but how can I coach others to bring their full selves forward unless I'm willing to do the same?

In the early months of the pandemic, I turned to energy work to manage everything that was coming up in my life. I also used it with clients; I don't think anything else would have helped during those draining times. Coaching works at the level of the mind. Minds are meant to connect with our bodies, spirits, and energy. We need to open up to something bigger than ourselves in order to truly be ourselves.

Energy work never ceases to surprise me. At the height of the pandemic, I saw people totally wiped out from the virus. People drained from juggling young kids and working from home. People afraid for their loved ones. Most of all, I saw exhaustion. Not just at a physical level but at all levels of the self. And so, in addition to coaching, I added meditation, journeying (a form of deeper meditation and breathing practice that takes you into your past to heal wounds), visualization, or other energy work into sessions with clients. Each time, clients would come out relaxed and uplifted with a renewed sense of energy. Energy medicine and coaching is a powerful combination. When we are aware of our four levels of perception and understand how they create our momentum, we can take control of our inner shifts—intentionally and repeatedly—to forge new inner pathways that bring our mind, body, spirit, and energy into alignment.

For me, this alignment has had a powerful impact on how I show up and has given me a better understanding of how the energy around me impacts me. I'm now more aware of energy shifts in relation to a person, place, or circumstance, which empowers me to make decisions with clarity and, I hope, wisdom.

Healing Yourself at the Energetic Level

Stress, emotional trauma, family troubles, career struggles, interpersonal conflict, and neglected self-care are some of the many things that can deplete the body's energy system. To restore energy and rebalance functionality, seek out methods and people who can help bring you internal peace.

If you're hesitant, I get it. It's true that energy work hasn't yet been proven. The evidence we have is purely anecdotal. That anecdotal evidence goes back generations, but still, it isn't scientific proof. And I understand that many people feel more secure in practices that have been proven and explained. We just aren't there yet.

What I say to clients is, "What's the worst that can happen?" The worst-case scenario is that you tried something new. Maybe it didn't have the impact you wanted, but now you know, and you can move on to something else. Maybe the experience just relaxes you, or you may experience tremendous shifts in a short period of time. Reiki, reflexology, acupuncture, emotional freedom techniques, theta healing, massage therapy, chakra cleansing, and other practices target the energetic and spiritual levels of self, helping you to heal and shift.

My personal and professional experience is that one energy session can feel as powerful as ten coaching sessions. And many of my clients have felt the same way. It's about changing the input to change the output.

If we don't do any work on ourselves, chances are we will keep traveling the same momentum tunnel for the rest of our lives. And if we have children, we'll be passing that same blueprint along for generations to come.

Sealing the Tunnel

When it comes to changing the direction of your life, it's important to close the door on your old patterns and habits. This is what it means to commit. It means stepping onto your new path with both feet, not keeping one foot on the old path "just in case." Whether you've gone the energy healing route or you've been able to enact shifts on your own, be intentional about sealing off any entrances to your old momentum tunnel.

Here's what it might sound like in your head to leave entrances open:

"I'm going to keep doing some work on the side for my old company in case this new business idea doesn't work out."

"I like the relationship I'm in, but you never know how these things will go. I'll keep my online dating profile just in case."

"I know I said I wanted to travel, but that big, exciting trip will cost a lot. Instead, I'll just book a few smaller trips close to home."

"I really want that promotion, and I know I'll have a good shot if I knock this project out of the park, but that would mean stepping back on some other things. I should just try to do all of it to be safe."

Without full commitment, energy is divided and will run dry. Success is unlikely, and most probably, the pull of that old momentum tunnel will be too strong.

Once you've determined what you really want for yourself, commit fully. Seal off those "emergency" entrances to your old tunnel and empower the fullness of your energy—of YOU—to work toward creating your world.

Here's what it might sound like in your head when working to seal off those entrances:

"I've made a financial plan for the year ahead, and I'm going to go full speed ahead with this new business idea."

"I like the relationship I'm in, and I want to make it work. I'm shutting down my old profiles."

"I want to travel, and this big trip feels exciting to me. I've saved up enough, and I'm doing it."

"I really want that promotion, so I'm committing to knocking this key project out of the park. I'll meet with my team/manager ASAP about handing off this additional work."

In these scenarios, you empower yourself to be fully present with both feet firmly planted on the path you want to take. You've sealed off those emergency entrances so that the force of that old tunnel can't pull you away.

Does this mean you're unsafe and have no choice but to succeed? Of course not! The Universe provides an endless supply of opportunities at all stages of life, as long as you are tuned into them. You can't travel a new path if you're keeping one foot on the old one. Like a rubber band, you'll eventually get stretched too far—and guess which path you'll spring back to? Seal those entrances. Commit.

Beyond the Work

In coaching, I always tell clients that much of the work also happens outside our sessions because that's when they take what they've learned, or the insights they've gained, and start putting it into action. It's the same with energy work. Imagine someone getting a clogged artery surgically cleared, then going right back to the lifestyle that caused the clog in the first place. Commitment must happen during the session and beyond.

We can't fix problems with the same mindset that created them. If you decide to give energy work a try, be prepared to feel an impact in the moment and continue the work afterward. It's like that first push to get your bike moving. It gets the momentum started, but you must do the pedaling to keep it going.

Your energy will always have an impact, so commit to being intentional. That will require doing things differently, stepping outside your comfort zone, and being open to possibility. Shift that energy. Give yourself that push to get a new momentum started and keep it going.

Energy is contagious, and when you consciously cultivate positive energy within yourself, you become intentional in the impact you have on the world around you. Remember, too, that just as you reflect your energetic self at all levels, so does everyone else. What may look like anger, arrogance, judgement, or other difficult energies may reflect deep wounds or generational patterns in their energetic self. Approach everyone with compassion, curiosity, and a strong connection to your own energy.

CEO of Your Life Coaching Tip:

Your past has already written the blueprint for your future, but it isn't written in stone. Do the work to tune into all four levels of perception and create the necessary shifts in your energetic self to change your momentum. That's how you take charge and write your future the way YOU want.

Speaking Your Truth in Professional Settings

In this chapter, I refer to workplaces, but a professional setting can also be a school (yours or your child's), political organization, religious group, volunteer committee, or any other setting where professionalism is expected.

By this point in the book, it should be clear just how important it is to your self-worth, self-acceptance, and self-authority that you fully honor Your truth. That goes for professional settings too.

That said, from frontline workers to C-level executives, nearly everyone I work with has the same fear: speaking their truth in the workplace. Having made my own journey toward full authenticity in the workplace, I am intimately familiar with that fear and anxiety that comes with vulnerability. Those first steps can be frightening. And I know how impactful it is—to yourself and others—when you fully own your truth.

You might be wondering how to start speaking your truth at work, say what needs to be said, and speak up when you see a problem. How does one voice their opinions openly and professionally? Is it possible? And do you *really* need to do it?

Why Truth is Hard in the Workplace

Respect is often viewed as treating someone like an authority figure. In childhood, authority is embodied by parents, teachers, or coaches—figures who call the shots and to whom children are expected to show respect through unquestioning obedience.

This becomes our understanding of how the world is. It is understandable that in the workplace, our childhood fear of speaking up can resurface. We don't want to get in trouble. We don't want to be judged. We don't want to upset anyone, make anyone angry, or have anyone think less of us.

The voices inside us that say not to rock the boat are our Saboteurs. They also tell us we're being respectful when we hold back our truth; that we are keeping ourselves safe, keeping the peace, being realistic, or whatever lies they tell to keep us in our comfort zones. But what if we stopped listening to them? What if, instead, we defined respect as treating people like human beings?

Instead of letting the Saboteurs speak, what if we said things to ourselves like . . .

"When I approach others as though their minds are open, I am respecting them."

"When I shed light on potential problems, I am respecting the people around me by assuming they are open to co-creating solutions."

"When I approach conflict from a place of curiosity, I am respecting others by understanding that they have an inner experience I know nothing about."

"When I take an issue to management or HR, I am respecting the organization by not allowing the issue to fester and become bigger."

"When I ask for clarity, I'm respecting my need to fully understand expectations and the organization's need for everyone to be on the same page."

"When I share my unique ideas or opinions, I am respecting myself, my colleagues, and the organization by bringing all parts of myself forward to do the best work I possibly can."

Our fear of speaking up comes from a valid place. It's what we *do* with the fear that matters most. Do we learn from it, or do we lead from it?

Learning from Fear versus Leading from Fear

When you lead from your fear, you let it make the decisions in your life. It guides your path. When you learn from it, you lead from your highest self. Your leader within is a perpetual learner, continuously striving to reach higher and higher levels through the lessons life has to bring. Face your fear head on and examine it from all sides. Meditate on it. Journal about it. Consider where it comes from and how it is serving you in life right now.

Ask yourself:

"Is the fear leading toward what I truly want, or is it holding me in status quo?"

"What outcome am I truly afraid of?"

"What story am I telling myself about why not to have this conversation?

Where there's fear, there's a part of you that needs to heal. Get curious about your own fears and learn from them. You can't change things by ignoring fear or trying to shove it aside. You create real change by leaning into what scares you.

What Happens When You Speak Your Truth at Work?

Truth always leads to more truth. That's why it is so important to speak our truth, especially at work. When you commit to speaking truth from a heart of peace—a heart that leads with curiosity, compassion, and courage, rather than blame, shame, and judgement—you free yourself from all those limiting beliefs and old patterns that have consistently held you back, and you create a safe space for others to bring their truth forward.

The more people speak their truth in a way that is respectful—remembering that respect means treating people as human beings—the more psychological safety is cultivated within the corporate culture.

What does it mean to have psychological safety at work? It means knowing that you, too, will be met with respect. It can mean, for example, that when you make a mistake, you feel confident owning it, knowing it will prompt a solutions-focused discussion, not punishment or shame. It can mean never thinking twice about sharing an idea because you know all ideas are met with respectful consideration. It can mean never wasting energy keeping yourself "safe" from blame, gossip, or any other toxic behaviors. It can mean asking for help or guidance without worrying that someone might question your competence.

When we feel safe to speak our truth, we are all able to move forward with courage and clarity.

When Speaking Your Truth Backfires

Let's say you start speaking your truth more and more at work. You do so respectfully and professionally, and it backfires. No one else is rising to meet you. The energy is shifting, and it isn't in a positive direction.

Isn't that a good thing? You deserve an environment that empowers you to thrive within the organization. That isn't selfishness or entitlement. That's a basic human need and of great value to any organization. Organizations are driven by the people within them, and they are most successful when they fully support those people.

If you start speaking your truth and it backfires, that's a very clear, very loud signal that this is not the organization for you and it's time to start planning your exit strategy. You may not be able to just quit and move on, and that's OK. Life needs to go on, bills need to be paid, families need to be supported. Just don't settle.

You may not be able to leave today, but that doesn't mean you can't get the ball rolling. Start exploring your options, fixing up your CV, expanding your skills and knowledge, and clarifying what you truly want. You cannot thrive where you cannot be YOU.

Let's look at some examples of how truth might backfire, and how you might respond to those situations in a way that serves you:

Example One

You say:

"I spotted a potential roadblock in this plan. I know a lot of work went into this, and I really want to see it succeed. Do you have a minute to hear my concerns?"

They respond:

"The time for concerns is long past. Just stick to the schedule. Got it?"

Your response:

"I understand. I'll email you, and you can decide where to go from there."

You are responsible for what you contribute, not for how people respond. You've spotted a potential problem, and you have a responsibility to your own integrity to bring those concerns forward. Putting things in writing ensures there's a record that you've done your due diligence.

Example Two

You say:

"We seem to be butting heads on this timeline. I know the company has a set goal for getting this done, and I see that you have some concerns about that. Tell me what you're experiencing."

They respond:

With a passive-aggressive, "No, it's fine. We'll just go with your plan."

Your response:

"Your concerns matter, and your insight is important to this project. I want to hear what you have to say. Let's set up a meeting to discuss it."

You are not responsible for anyone else advocating for themselves. However, if you are held to a timeline, and someone has concerns, you have a responsibility to hear those concerns. Be firm and decisive.

Example Three

You say:

"I know the company is going through a challenging time, and I want to be a part of working through that. The problem is, I've been putting in too many evening and weekend hours. I feel like I'm burning out, and I can't bring my best to this role without time to recharge. Can we discuss some options?"

They respond:

"I know things are tough, but there isn't any wiggle room right now. Let's come back to this next quarter."

Your response:

"I appreciate that, but I have to consider my own well-being. Can we talk on Monday?"

Unfortunately, deflection is a common tactic when managers want to keep the peace but also have no intention of hearing, or responding to, your needs. Push for an earlier conversation. If they still deflect, see if there's someone else in the company you can talk to, such as someone in HR. Keep it professional and avoid burning bridges, but advocate for yourself and know that leaving the organization may be the best thing for your health.

Example Four

You say:

"When I had the chance to partner with the other department a few weeks ago, I felt really energized by the work they're doing. I think I might have a lot to contribute, and I wonder if you would be open to my partnering with them again and perhaps growing my career in that direction long term."

They respond:

"Why? Aren't you happy here?"

Your response:

"I've learned so much in this team under your leadership. Now I feel ready to grow in different directions. What guidance can you give me?"

Territorialism is common in unhealthy work environments. Some leaders might think it reflects poorly on them if people leave the team, or they might not want to share good talent. Regardless, you deserve opportunities to grow. When you find yourself in a conversation with someone's ego, asking for their help or expertise can be a powerful tactic—if, and only if, it helps you get out from under them.

Example Five

You say:

"I've been thinking about the vision I hold for the organization and want to ensure it is fully aligned with the corporate vision. Do you have a moment to help me get clarity?"

They respond:

"Listen, vision is great, but we need to focus on the tasks in front of us. You have an assignment, that's all you need to know."

Your response:

Busy-ness without a big picture vision isn't productivity. It's just running on a hamster wheel. And yet, so many people—even in leadership—get too caught up in getting things done to understand the value of a vision and its role in achieving objectives. Consider if there's someone else in the organization that you can have an informal conversation with in order to get clarity. If there are in-house resources on goal setting or career development, take advantage of those. If your leader isn't willing to support you, be your own leader.

Example Six

You say:

"I had an idea. From my perspective, it's in line with our objectives for this year, but I realize I may have blind spots I'm not aware of. Can I get your feedback on it?"

They respond:

Let's say they give you a fifteen-minute time slot. They hear your idea and all they say is something like, "I'll give it some thought," then

157

rush you out. This isn't the first time, and you know from experience that you're likely to be ignored. Being open to other people's ideas isn't the norm in this organization.

Your response:

You may really need to gauge the environment and your idea. Is this a situation where you could just start working on your ideas, without explicit leadership support? Do you have colleagues you feel you could team up with? If not, start working on your CV. An environment that stifles ingenuity will only sap your energy and wear you down.

You'll notice that these conversation openers are rooted in curiosity and open to possibility. When we use phrases like, "You always disagree with me," or "That won't work," or "I can't work like this anymore," we shut down possibilities. We draw a line in the sand that puts others on the defensive. You aren't a safe space but are someone to stay safe from. The curiosity approach, on the other hand, is confident, strong, compassionate, co-creative, respectful, and professional. It also reflects well on you as a team player.

Eleven Tips and Mindset Shifts to Prepare for Workplace Truth

One. Remember that you were hired in your role for a reason. That includes your skills, qualities, experience, and perspective. Staying quiet does not honor the strengths you were chosen for.

Two. Fear is normal. Confront your fear and learn from it so that it has no power to lead you. Learning from fear and leading from truth is how change is created.

Three. Embrace conflict because conflict itself is not the real enemy. Avoiding conflict is. When you learn to embrace conflict as a growth opportunity, it starts to lose some of the fear it usually brings with it and empowers you and those around you to truly move forward. Conflict is growth.

Four. Ask yourself, "What story am I telling myself that's holding me in status quo?" Write the story out if it helps you get clarity. Then ask, "How can I retell this story in an empowering way?"

Five. Forget about the consequences. The fact is, you don't know how your truth will be received. You might fear your boss will think you're incompetent if you ask for clarity, but often it sends the message that you're truly invested in aligning your efforts with corporate vision and objectives. Your unique idea might not be put into practice, but it will give others the opportunity to look at things from a different perspective and see even more possibilities. Your boss might be busy and overscheduled but will likely welcome the opportunity to connect and get insight into how things are really going. And if your truth isn't welcomed with respect . . . is that really the environment you want to spend your precious energy on?

Six. Be intentional. Intentionally create new rituals and routines for yourself in order to embed any new skill into your daily life. Hiding your truth is simply a habit—an old pattern that can be broken and replaced.

Seven. Give mindfulness and meditation a genuine try. Speaking your truth can take a lot of emotional energy in the moment. Regular mindfulness and meditation practices keep your emotional energy fueled up and train your brain to notice what's coming up in the moment, so that you can respond consciously, rather than react unconsciously.

Eight. Tune into your gut. Our bodies will often alert us to our truth before our brains are consciously aware of it. When something shifts or twinges in your body, take a moment with that feeling. What is it trying to tell you?

Nine. Be open to change and disagreement. Your truth is not everyone else's. Just as your truth is worthy of respect, their truth is worthy of respect.

Ten. Stretch yourself in non-conflict moments. It's even harder to create a new habit if you only practice it when the stress is high, so commit to stretching your new "truth muscles" in the everyday moments. This will help train those muscles so that when the need for truth is highest, you have built up the strength to step into it.

Eleven. Get comfortable with being uncomfortable. The fact is, truth feels vulnerable. It's open, raw, and not shrouded in all our self-protective habits and patterns. When someone is unkind in the face of our truth, it can hurt deeply. But here's another fact: it hurts a lot less, and for a much shorter time, than the persistent pain of shoving our truth aside day after day, year after year.

Have you ever watched someone fix a car? It's a messy, greasy process—parts everywhere, sections taken apart—until the problem is fixed, the mess is cleaned up, and the car is running smoothly again. Mess is nothing to fear if you're willing to see it through. Take full responsibility for your world. Your truth opened a can of worms? Good.

It probably needed to happen. Now stay with it. Help sort through the muck and clean up.

As humans, we learn through our lived experiences, and we are all in various states of growth and change. Respect in all areas of life—work included—demands that we honor the human experience. Commit to creating a new lived experience for yourself—one that grows you in the direction of empowerment and self-leadership.

> ### CEO of Your Life Coaching Tip:
>
> Often, it's where we're most afraid to speak our truth that we most NEED to speak our truth. It's where we most need to bring our shadow into the light. The problem is, most of us were never taught how to speak our truth in professional settings. Lean into that. This is just a new skill to learn. And, like any new skill, there will be a learning curve.

Authoring Your Mental Models

A great deal of becoming You is changing the way you think. I want to be clear: changing the way you think is not about changing who you are. It's about building awareness of where your thoughts come from, and what they are reacting to, so you can consciously and intentionally cultivate a mindset that is inherently You.

In this chapter, we're going to explore mental models as a way of understanding how you relate to the people and situations around you, how you *want* to relate to them, and a very practical tool to help you shift into action.

What Are Mental Models and How Do They Impact You?

Mental models are your thought processes. They are built out of all your experiences, assumptions, beliefs, old patterns, and so on. You already have mental models, whether you're aware of them or not, and they are highly influential in how you show up and respond to your environment and circumstances.

Have you ever worked with a computer system and wanted it to do something, but it just wouldn't cooperate? Mental models can be a lot like that, especially when we aren't aware of them. We want to show up in a different way, but it's like our brain is returning an error message. Just like a computer or piece of software can be reprogrammed, however, you can reprogram your mind with updated mental models. The "reprogram your thoughts" exercise from earlier is a great starting point. Here, we're going to dig deeper with a tool you can tailor to almost any situation in order to shift your mental models and better understand how other people's mental models drive their behavior.

Why Do Mental Models Have Such a Hold on Us?

There is a lot we don't know about how human thinking evolved and why it evolved the way it did. But I ask you to consider this: much of human evolution has been oriented towards maximizing our chances at survival. What if that's how thinking evolved as well? What if our minds have evolved to fear difficult or painful interactions as a survival mechanism? It would make sense that, when our brains sense a potentially threatening situation, they hold us back from engaging.

What are we likely to see as threatening?

Conflict

Disagreement

Voicing our needs

Sharing different ideas

Speaking our truth

Standing up for ourselves or others

Sharing our experience

Saying what we want

These things can feel scary. When we are afraid, we either avoid the issue or approach it aggressively so that we are "protected" right from the start.

We need to give our evolution a little nudge if we want to intentionally override that programming. By educating ourselves on our own mental models, we can make powerful, intentional shifts that help our brains to better understand a genuine threat versus an uncomfortable interaction.

Identifying Your Mental Models

Identifying your mental models can be as simple as filling in a worksheet. At the end of this book in the resources section, is an image of a mental model worksheet, which you can also download as a printable sheet from my website.

Here's how to use the sheet:

One. Be clear and granular on the subject.

Whether it's a decision to be made, a problem to be solved, an idea to share, or a disagreement to work through, be clear on the issue you're approaching. Enter the problem into the "Subject to Explore" section. Get granular. For example, imagine you don't feel right about a new policy at work. What, specifically, do you not feel right about? Drill down to the exact point (or points).

Two. Determine who else is involved.

In a workplace setting, the "who" can be an individual or a full team. In a personal setting, it could be an individual, your family, a social group, etc. Be aware that groups, families, and teams often function as complete systems with their own personalities, beliefs, expectations, and value systems. In complex groups like families, even if your issue is with the whole group, it might make sense to consider each individual separately, as each relationship will have its own nuances. With professional or community groups, where relationships are less complex, it might make sense to approach the group as a single entity.

Three. Get curious about your truth.

In the "My Truth" row, there are five categories with questions and prompts to help you excavate what's going on for you. Start with the basic facts. The other four categories can be done in any order, but it is vital to get clear on the subject and facts first to help you stay on topic.

When filling in the facts, avoid using qualifiers. For example, instead of, "When I bring up [subject], I am immediately shut down, and that's making it impossible to communicate," simply write, "When I bring up [subject], I am immediately shut down." That is your fact, as you know it. The part about communication also matters but is more of a personal thought or belief. Instead, you could put that in the "Thoughts" category, as, "I think this is making communication impossible between us." Or you could place it in the "Beliefs & Expectations" category, as, "I expect us to be able to share thoughts more openly, and I believe this issue is making that impossible."

Use "I" statements as much as possible.

Four. Get curious about their truth, as you know it.

You can't know for sure what's happening for them, but this is an opportunity to shift your mind into "possibility mode" and start exploring all sides of the subject. What might be coming up for the other person? What facts might they have that you don't? What facts might be more important to them than they are to you? What values might this touch on for them? What might someone in their position be thinking or feeling?

Five. Explore the potential of "Us Together."

For this section, think about how both sides can be brought together. Where can you be flexible without compromising what's most important to you? What common ground can you co-create from? What might they be willing to compromise on? What expectations, thoughts or feelings might be holding you back that you can work through?

Remember, you aren't creating the solution here. At this stage, you're opening your own mind, getting a clear picture of your mental model, and taking full responsibility for how you show up and respond.

What Next?

Just by going through the worksheet, you've already taken a practical step toward shifting your mental models. You've built awareness of your current models and have gotten curious about different perspectives and possibilities.

Now ask yourself:

What have I gained through this awareness?

In what ways was my old mental model holding me back?

How will I use my new awareness to move forward?

A Note on Privilege

When it comes to interpersonal differences, it's important to be aware of when you might be in a position of privilege and explore how that may be impacting your mental models. For example, you may see the solution to a community issue as very simple. But, if you only see it from a perspective of privilege, there are likely many issues you aren't seeing, and haven't factored into your solution.

When it comes to privilege, listening and curiosity are vital, as is compassion for how others show up. If the other person seems combative to you, consider that they might have spent a lifetime fighting to be heard. If they are adamant that your perspective is wrong, consider that you may have blind spots you're unaware of. Really hear what's being said and *believe* their experience. We can all have different experiences that are *true for us*. Believing someone else's experience is only threatening if there's something in *your world* that needs to shift.

If the situation is reversed and it's the other person in a position of privilege, remember that you are not responsible for shifting their mental models. You are only responsible for You. Show up in your truth. Lean on your support system (or seek out a strong support system/person). Your truth matters. If you feel safe doing so, you can end a conversation with, "I've heard what you have to say. You are not hearing me. I'm ending this conversation until you're ready to listen."

Using Mental Model Awareness to Move Forward in Truth

What you do next will depend on the specifics of the issue; what you have determined matters most to you; and the new perspectives, curiosity, and flexibility you have created for yourself. Sometimes, you might realize it was enough to do this inner exploration and you don't need to have an actual conversation. Maybe you've realized the issue was mainly rooted in your mental model and/or how you'd been showing up. In that case, it's best to do the work you need to do, then revisit the issue to see if there's anything remaining to work through.

If you do determine that a conversation is worth having, here are four approaches to consider:

One. Bring your worksheet to the other person.

You've gone through a meaningful process. Why not share that? Show the other person where you started, what your concerns are, what matters to you, your thoughts about their perspective, and areas in which you feel you can be flexible. Try something like: "I've been thinking over this issue, and I'd like to share my thought process with you. I'd like us to create something that works for both of us."

Two. Have both of you complete the worksheet separately, then come together.

If you feel the other person would be receptive, suggest you each complete your own worksheets separately so that when you come together, each party's point of view is clearly outlined, and you can start building mutual understanding. Try something like: "I'd like to get a conversation going on this. I imagine we each have different values at play and objectives to consider, but I also think we can find some common ground to create from. Would you be open to a little exercise that will help us both be heard and understand each other better?"

Three. Break the ice with vulnerability.

Vulnerability is a powerful quality to embrace. When you show up from a vulnerable place—meaning a place with no armor, personas, or self-protective habits—you immediately become non-threatening, which can help disarm that knee-jerk reaction in others to shut down. Try something like: "It's difficult for me to have this conversation. I'm not used to speaking up, and I'm still getting comfortable with openness." Unless the person you're dealing with is truly toxic, chances are they have the same very human fears and awkward feelings. Vulnerability levels the playing field. It puts you on an equal footing where co-creation can thrive.

Four. Invite collaboration.

When you fill out the worksheet, you are forced to make assumptions about the other person's perspective. Lean into that to invite collaboration. Feeling heard and valued matters to everyone—even your boss! When you invite someone in with curiosity, you show them, from the start, that you want to hear them and that you value their truth. Try something like: "I really want to get your perspective on this because I know I'm only seeing it from my point of view right now. How do you see it? What am I missing that you can fill in?" Then really listen as they speak. Does what they're saying differ from your original assumptions? If so, how can you continue to be flexible? How else can you bridge the gap? What else is possible?

Mental models are strong but not fixed. Through awareness, you can build flexibility into your mental models. When your thought processes are flexible and you are confidently aligned with your values, the idea of speaking your truth becomes less threatening. In this state, you know you lose nothing in speaking up, even if your truth is disagreed with. Like anything else, it gets easier and less frightening with practice. Commit to seeing each effort as a stepping stone.

One of my mantras is that truth always brings more truth. Everyone around you is waiting for a safe space to allow their own truth to emerge. When you start sharing yours from a place of curiosity, you become that safe space.

> **CEO of Your Life Coaching Tip:**
>
> Mental models are strong but not fixed. When you commit to building your awareness, intentionally creating new patterns, and retraining your mind to see others through a lens of curiosity, you open so many possibilities for yourself and those around you. What conflict, ongoing disagreement, or tense relationship can you commit to exploring today?

YOU as an Ally

Imagine a bunch of different ingredients—flour, baking powder, sugar, salt, eggs, milk, butter—each with their own unique properties. Those unique properties have value on their own, but it's when they're integrated that they bring the full force of that value forward. When combined, they co-create something wonderful (in this example, pancakes!).

People are not pancake ingredients. But we are all unique, each with our own strengths, talents, knowledge, experience, perspectives, and passions that bring value to ourselves, our families, our workplaces, our communities, and our friend circles.

When we are not secure in our own self-worth, differences in others can feel threatening. That's when our minds are closed to our own blind spots and areas of privilege. That's when we see efforts to empower another person or group and think, "But what about me?" It's when we recognize injustice but think someone else will handle it. It's when we tell ourselves "That's got nothing to do with me," or "I can't make a difference on my own, so why try?"

When you fully step into your self-worth and accept and honor the humanity in yourself and others, you begin to see that you not only have a responsibility to the world in how you show up, but you also have the capacity to create positive change in the world. Simply by taking responsibility for how you show up, you can completely turn your world on its head. While you may not be able to completely turn the WHOLE world on its head, you absolutely can be a powerful agent of change and an important ally to others.

Value in Action

When I coach organizations and professional leaders, I sometimes start with that simplistic pancake analogy to get us all in that same mindset of diversity having value. In business, as in life, diversity matters because each of us has something to contribute. When we take full advantage of those contributions, we co-create incredible things.

True diversity—not just hiring practices but fully integrating and uplifting everyone's contribution instead of expecting assimilation—can be especially challenging in systems where even a little bit of "different" thinking is frowned upon. I've noticed similar struggles in families and communities where fitting in is a question of survival, either figuratively or literally.

When I talk to business leaders about creating workplace cultures that welcome, empower, and integrate diversity, I spend a lot of time on what it truly means to value diversity—to put value into action. Here are some examples of what that looks like:

Openly recognizing contributions.

Holding authentic conversations.

Asking for input and advice.

Taking all opinions into consideration.

Getting curious about strengths, interests, and passions, especially beyond the job description.

Constructive feedback.

Active listening.

Interest in, and guidance for, professional and personal development.

Showing up from a place of curiosity and compassion.

Embracing conflict as an opportunity for better understanding.

Owning your own assumptions and taking full responsibility for shifting them.

It is primarily intangible actions—behaviors and practices baked into the culture—that tell people whether they are genuinely valued. These practices can look similar in our personal lives as well. When you fully embrace and honor the human in all of us, you recognize that your own comfort zones and assumptions are your responsibility and that to truly value yourself and everyone around you, you need to seize that responsibility.

YOU as an Ally

Gandhi famously said to "be the change you want to see in the world." What that means is to CREATE the change.

Inequality and exclusion exist in so many areas of life. They're baked into mindsets, policies, social structures, laws, and so on. Just as those structures were created intentionally by humans, they can all be changed intentionally by humans. To be an ally means you actively work against the structures that leave others out, recognizing that you lose nothing by doing so. This *can* mean attending protests, volunteering, donating, or fundraising; but most importantly, it means speaking up when you become aware of someone being treated as less human than someone else.

For you, that could mean telling a family member you will no longer tolerate their bigoted comments, and if they continue, you will end your relationship with them. It could mean standing up for a coworker in the face of an irate customer *and* continuing to support them beyond the experience. It could mean writing letters to news outlets when they show bias in their reporting. It means anytime you see injustice, you call it out. That voice inside that tries to tell you not to make waves or that it's not worth it because you can't change anything, that's your Saboteurs trying to shove things into your shadow. Bring it all out. Let your leader within guide you.

Creating a Sense of Belonging

Everyone has their own unique experience. You may not be able to fully understand the inner experience of everyone from every background, and that's OK. What you *can* understand is what exclusion feels like.

At some point in our lives, even if it was way back in childhood on the playground, we have all had an experience of not belonging. We know that it can bring feelings of fear, sadness, isolation, anger, and resentment. To not belong or feel accepted and worthy as you are is an awful feeling.

Hopefully, you also have experience of what it feels like to belong or have someone who is a safe space for you. Commit to being someone who creates belonging and acts as a safe space of acceptance and respect for others. Whether it's a colleague, family member, or neighbor, when you recognize someone may not feel safe or feel like they belong, be a safe space of belonging.

Adopt an Abundance Mindset

A candle can light a thousand other candles without losing any of its own light. When you have done the inner work to fully step into You, you can truly feel, deep within, that you lose nothing by lifting someone else. If anything, you gain even more light in your life.

As someone who spent many years in the marketing industry, I can tell you that the media is full of messages of scarcity. It's a tactic to create demand and a sense that you're constantly in competition with others; that if you don't get it first, someone else will snap it up. The problem is that this plays into people's real fears that there isn't enough to go around, and it even gets used on a political level to convince people that other groups are trying to take from them.

None of that is true. There is enough of everything in the world for everyone. A big part of what fuels inequality is this fearful mindset of scarcity.

When it comes to how you use the awesomeness within you, adopt a mindset of abundance. You can share your joy, compassion, courage, laughter, love, and respect with every single person around you and lose none of it for yourself in the process. It is all endlessly renewable and grows the more you give it away.

Five Ways to Show Up in Allyship

These are five tips that I share with organizations, modified to apply to everyday life:

One—Prioritize authenticity.

When you are authentic, you recognize where your knowledge or experience may be lacking. You listen when others speak. You own your privilege and actively seek to identify and illuminate your own blind spots. You admit your mistakes and recognize that mistakes in others are human, acceptable, and a natural part of every journey forward.

Two—Assume a mindset of "anything is possible."

It's so common to get caught in that "this is just the way it's done" mindset. Especially in times of chaos or unrest. But that's how you get stuck and growth stalls. Be intentional about adopting an "anything is possible" mindset. When you are secure in You and what you want to create, you recognize that true progress only happens when you are open to all possibilities.

Three—Value the whole person, not just their direct contribution.

Yes, we all have unique gifts, strengths, and talents to contribute, but we are all more than what we give. Each of us is born with value simply by virtue of being human. Recognize that. No one owes you or anyone else their gifts, and no one should ever have to prove their value as a human being. You matter because you are here. That is enough.

Four—Establish an internal coaching and mentorship program.

With organizations, I guide them to focus not just on diverse hiring practices but to take an honest look at how people progress and grow within the organization. Creating internal programs that offer advancement and growth opportunities for everyone is key to cultivating inclusivity, as well as creating stronger and more diverse interpersonal relationships.

What does that look like in everyday life? Look at the institutions in which you belong. This could be a workplace, school, extended family, community organization, or religious group, any collection of people. How can you be of service? How can you lift others up? What can you do to open opportunities for others?

Maybe you can offer to do a weekly grocery run for someone who struggles with mobility or can't afford transportation. Maybe you can offer tutoring services. Maybe you can reach out to someone you sense may be feeling isolated.

Remember that you don't have to fill your cup just to serve others. Be mindful of your own boundaries and generous with the abundance of what you do have to give.

Five—Lead from a heart of peace.

Many of us *want* to welcome all ideas and perspectives and *want* to be allies. So why aren't we doing it? One reason is that we may not be conscious of how much our behaviors and actions aren't coming from our true selves.

From a young age, most of us are taught that fitting in is better than standing out. We then bring that mentality into our adult lives, limit ourselves and everyone around us, and hide our shadows, leading from hearts of war that keep us in defense mode. Embracing a heart of peace means identifying your limiting beliefs and cutting them off at the root so that You can thrive. When you do that, you can lead yourself and others from a place of genuine authenticity, vulnerability, and courage.

This is how you become a safe space for others to drop their own defenses. When you step into You and take full responsibility for how you show up, your energy will ripple out, changing the world in ways you may never even know about. Being You is about so much more than your own interior experiences. It's about recognizing that each one of us creates the world around us and that not everyone is working with the same materials in that creative process.

When the pandemic began, many people were using the expression, "We're all in the same boat." That was quickly corrected to understanding that we may all be in the same storm, but we are absolutely in different boats. When you see someone struggling in the storm—or even struggling in the calm—ask yourself how you can make a difference. What can you give? Who can you alert? What barriers can you break down? Who or what can you stand up to?

> **CEO of Your Life Coaching Tip:**
>
> A candle loses none of its light by lighting another. Forget about what you can't do and focus on how you can show up in a way that creates safe space and positive change for you and everyone around you.

It's YOUR Journey

This book began with the day I became an Amazon international best seller. What should have been a moment of joy ended in tears.

Those tears were a gift.

The hurtful comments I received started me on a healing journey that brought me to a state of wholeness where I can just be Me. I have taken back the power that's rightfully mine and no longer let others author my life. I am firmly seated in my own CEO chair and no longer feel any obligation to pass it to others or to occupy theirs. I own what's mine and only what's mine. When I get off track, I have the tools, strengths, and healthy boundaries to get back on.

Unfortunately, we don't go through life without pain. I took my painful experiences, one by one, and examined them from all sides. I dropped the masks created from those experiences and stepped into myself with love and acceptance.

And now I want the same for you.

I know this is not an easy process. In the depths of my pain, I leaned on my healer and coach for strength. What I came to understand is that my first book reflected who I was at the time. Likewise, the judgment from others reflected them, not me.

If I were to rewrite that book today, of course it would be different. I have grown as a person. I'm not who I was in that time and space. In two or three years, I might look back at this book and say I could have done it differently. I accept that. I'm in a place where I can fully accept, with love, that I may be wrong. I may make mistakes. I am human, and I am enough.

We are always works in progress. We need to be kind and patient with ourselves as we evolve. If you feel stuck or run down or like things need to change, ask yourself, "Where can I *grow* from here?" Growing implies you must learn the way. It's compassionate, inspiring, and courageous to choose growth over running in place.

I was talking with my friend Jay, a filmmaker, recording artist, and singer-songwriter. He told me that some artists rush to get their albums out because they feel each new project is so much better than the previous one. Those words really resonated with me.

Initially, I was in such a hurry to get this book out to "make up" for the first one, but that mindset makes the past seem like nothing but mistakes instead of the growth journey that it is. To sit fully in my own self-worth means love and acceptance of all aspects of myself at all *times* of myself.

Since publishing that book, I have put great distance between the old Me and the Me of today. The Me of today is aligned with her true character and more powerful than I ever imagined possible. I love her, just as I love every version of Me who came before and made today's Me possible.

When we put our truth out there—whether in a book, conversation, career path, hobby, or parenting—our work is always subjective. In embracing vulnerability, we honor ourselves and hopefully inspire others to honor themselves.

Aside from the few naysayers, I also had countless people tell me they felt the book was their story or that it had been written just for them—that it inspired them to do something different and more fulfilling for themselves. Those are the reviews I keep going back to because those are the people I was writing for.

As you move forward on your own journey, as you begin to do things differently and rock the boat a little, you will get pushback. People who see you a certain way and expect certain things from you will likely be uncomfortable with your change. That is their work to do, not yours. Don't let their limits hold you back. Instead of giving in to the will of others, taking things personally, and giving away pieces of yourself, remind yourself of this: Whatever someone is saying or doing is only a reflection of where they are, not where you are. Don't give your power away and don't break yourself into pieces for anyone else's comfort. Be You. Own what's yours and only what's yours.

In my first book, *I Attract What I Am*, I wrote about my relationships. At that time in my life, they were my criteria for moving forward. My relationships, for better or worse, made me grow and propelled me onto my personal growth and coaching path. The failures I experienced helped me look into myself, want more, and do better for myself.

Relationships can teach you what makes you tick, and it's in your power to decide what to do with those lessons. What you give and what you accept can tell you a lot about where you are right now and show you what you need to work on. When a relationship no longer serves you, when it holds you back from You, it's healthy to let it go. You learned, and now it's time to move on.

Since the writing of my first book I have learned, the hard way, that the answer doesn't lie in anyone but Me. The answer—to everything—is to fall in love with, nurture, and honor yourself as the deeply worthy human being that you are, despite what anyone says. When you do this, you become so happy and emit such a positive vibration that it attracts people at an even higher vibration. We're not meant to go it alone, but we aren't meant to give away our power either.

What I needed to understand, at my core, was that it was an important part of my journey to inspire the people my first book attracted. Those people were ready to hear that message and appreciated my vulnerability. Others did not appreciate my message. Either they needed to heal in certain areas of their lives, or they weren't ready for the message I was sharing. And that's OK. I know now their reactions were not a reflection of me or my journey.

The thing is, that book is not my whole story. And neither is this one. These are just chapters in my life. There will always be more chapters and more roads on my map.

Whatever your story is today, it is only your story if you continue to tell it that way. You may not have created everything that happened to you, but you have cultivated the way you tell the story, which impacts the way it will continue to unfold. Reimagine your story. Look at what you can learn or grow from in your past, what you have accomplished, and what strengths are within you. Choose to make these elements the theme of your story. A CEO is always open to new ways of growing in the direction of what they want to create. When you choose to be the CEO of your life—the Hero of your own story—you choose personal growth. You choose to be continually learning, growing, challenging yourself, and bringing the best YOU forward.

As Socrates said, "To find yourself, think for yourself." The cost of not being You is your self-worth. That's too high a cost. Explore yourself. Become yourself. Accept yourself. Approve of yourself.

Do your inner work and shatter the old programs keeping you stuck. Set your boundaries and hold them with love. Learn to let go and be kind, gentle, and compassionate with yourself, every step of the way. Discover (or create) your reason for being and go for it, full steam ahead. Reclaim your power—your inherent right to author your life story. Know that going your own way does not mean going it alone. Embrace real support that uplifts and respects you.

Always re-evaluate where you are. Everything that has happened to date was designed to be that way, or you would not be becoming the amazing person that you are, so keep checking in with yourself. Something that was good in the past can be harmful for you now. Work with a coach, healer, or therapist to ensure all your incremental changes are aligned with You.

Say this to yourself: "I have come to peace. I accept and love that I am a rule breaker and a front runner. I carve my own way of being. This is my light; this is my truth."

I hope this book inspired you to step into your light. To love it and to shine it. To shine it so strong that people around you feel good with you and feel they can be their true selves too.

May the wounds you want to heal not bring you down. May they instead light the way to unwrapping the You that exists beneath them. And then, may your gifts shine brightly into the world.

Keep writing your beautiful story.

Bye-bye to people-pleasing. Hello, being YOU.

CEO of Your Life Coaching Tip:

Remember, always, that what's in your heart is meant to come forward. It is your truest self, and it is your best self. Take those brave steps. Drop the masks and be YOU. Bravely and unapologetically.

Appendix

CEO of Your Life Coaching Tips

Chapter 1

No matter how hard things get, don't let negativity hold you back. Continually ask yourself questions that enable new possibilities in every situation.

Chapter 2

Where do you need to take a stand in your life? Listen to that voice inside you. What step can you take—however small—that is led by your heart, not other people's opinions?

Chapter 3

You don't have to keep carrying beliefs that someone else handed you. Keep asking yourself, "Is this belief truly mine? Is it serving me? Do I want to keep carrying it, or can I shed it?"

Chapter 4

Opportunity will always come knocking. It's up to you to decide if You answer, or if you let your fear, hurt, and limiting beliefs answer. When you make the choice to drop your mask and open that door as your truest, most vulnerable self, you begin to create true, heartfelt connection that empowers genuine shifts in your life and the lives of those around you.

Chapter 5

You are already authoring your own story, and the only thing holding you back from writing yourself as the hero is you. Commit to taking full responsibility for YOUR world, starting now.

Chapter 6

Your leader within is You. Tune into it. Trust in your inner GPS. This is the path to truly honoring and being You.

Chapter 7

Your shadow is part of You and is worthy of full acceptance. As you practice accepting your own shadow, set the intention to accept the shadow in others as well. Accept that the people around you will make mistakes. They will say and do things that seem hurtful to you but

WHY CAN'T I JUST BE ME?

may not have anything to do with you. You can set healthy boundaries around hurtful behavior AND respect the person on the other side.

Chapter 8

Life is in the details. Commit to becoming conscious of the rituals, habits and practices holding you where you are today and consciously creating new ones that nourish You. Work on your energy. Try different things until you find what works for you. Recognize your wounds and embrace them with love and acceptance. Give your body what it needs. Refuel in nature. Eat healthy foods to help you show up as your best self. Above all, put yourself in charge of how you show up every day.

Chapter 9

The wisdom in your body is your bridge to life around you and your path to healing the fragmentation of mind and body. Don't ignore or discredit the messages your body is telling you. They are coming up for a reason and deserve your attention. Meditation is a practice that guides us to reconnect our bodies and minds with intention. Consider trying a few different approaches to meditation to see if there is a good fit for you.

Chapter 10

Real progress happens when you are clear on what you're working toward. Having a life purpose statement and vision of what you want to create empowers you to make choices that propel you in the direction you want to go.

Chapter 11

A heart of war can mean you're on the offensive or defensive, triggered by self-preservation mode. A defensive heart isn't looking for a fight but desperately trying to avoid one and can't help but see everything and everyone around it as obstacles to overcome. Work within to connect with your heart and bring it into a state of peace. From a heart of peace comes infinite possibility.

Chapter 12

Your state of being is yours to determine. Tap into habits and practices that put you, repetitively, into the CEO seat of your own life.

Chapter 13

To end the draining, people-pleasing cycle, you need healthy boundaries—a place where you can love yourself fully while honoring and respecting the other person. You have to put up walls against situations and people that cause you to feel less than whole. You are responsible for your wholeness and yours alone. Trust that others will find their own way if, and when, they're ready. And if you're a parent, remember that setting your own healthy boundaries and respecting your children's boundaries sets a loving example that will continue for generations.

Chapter 14

Every relationship has one element that you can fully control: You. In fact, it's the only element you fully control. If you have a relationship that is troubling you, or that you want to take to the next level, turn your perspective back onto yourself. How can you author your next steps in a way that you are your own hero, advocating for yourself and owning your self-worth?

Chapter 15

Embracing confrontation is essential to progress and well-being and keeps you firmly in the CEO seat of your life. Partner with confrontation, prepare yourself for who you are about to confront, and approach the conversation with peace and curiosity.

Chapter 16

Pour your heart out through a pen. Speak from where and when the hurt happened. Writing will help you release unhealthy emotions and unexpressed words and let go of what could have/should have been. If you feel you need more help processing your emotions and healing your wounds, talk with a coach, healer, or therapist you trust.

Chapter 17

Your past has already written the blueprint for your future, but it isn't written in stone. Do the work to tune into all four levels of perception and create the necessary shifts in your energetic self to change your momentum. That's how you take charge and write your future the way YOU want.

Chapter 18

Often, it's where we're most afraid to speak our truth that we most NEED to speak our truth. It's where we most need to bring our shadow into the light. The problem is, most of us were never taught how to speak our truth in professional settings. Lean into that. This is just a new skill to learn. And, like any new skill, there will be a learning curve.

Chapter 19

Mental models are strong but not fixed. When you commit to building your awareness, intentionally creating new patterns, and retraining your mind to see others through a lens of curiosity, you open so many possibilities for yourself and those around you. What conflict, ongoing disagreement, or tense relationship can you commit to exploring today?

Chapter 20

A candle loses none of its light by lighting another. Forget about what you can't do and focus on how you can show up in a way that creates safe space and positive change for you and everyone around you.

Chapter 21

Remember, always, that what's in your heart is meant to come forward. It is your truest self, and it is your best self. Take those brave steps. Drop the masks and be YOU. Bravely and unapologetically.

CEO of Your Life Reflections

Chapter 5 - Do you feel you are taking responsibility for your world? If not, what would it look like if you did?

Chapter 6 - Think about an area of your life where you need to make a decision. Imagine the different options in front of you. One by one, visualize yourself moving forward with each path, including how the outcome will look and feel. Really let yourself feel, with your whole body, the energy of that choice and its outcome. What outcome feels lightest in your body? If the outcome feels light, but the path itself feels heavy, what might you be afraid to face? What can you do, or who can you turn to, to help you along that path to lightness?

Chapter 9 - Does your physical space reflect the true You and what you want to create for yourself? What gets repeated gets remembered. Harness that power by choosing three things you can change in your environment today or this week to align your purpose and vision.

Free Resources

Six Steps to Unleash Your Inner Leader
There is a leader inside all of us. A leader that helps us bring out the best of ourselves, in all areas of life, and inspires those around us to elevate themselves as well. When you unleash your inner leader, you take yourself, your team, your organization, your family, your community, and your world to the next level.

In this free guide, you will get exercises and tips to:

- Determine your core values.

- Provide you with direction and clarity.

- Be true to who you really are.

https://ceoofyour.life/inner-leader

Personal Assessment Wheel
https://ceoofyour.life/wp-content/uploads/2021/11/Assessment-Wheel-Heart-Illumination-2.pdf

Mental Models Worksheet
https://ceoofyour.life/wp-content/uploads/2021/11/Fillable-form-CEO_mental-models-worksheet.pdf

Acknowledgments

I would like to thank my family, who set up the environment that led me to be who I am today.

I am so grateful to my son. Let's face it: life has ups and downs. When things got really down, he was the reason I picked myself up. I want to be the best mom possible for him. I want to show him that, no matter how tough things get, you can always turn them around. He is a wise soul. He has taught me a lot and continues to do so.

I would like to thank my amazing partner for believing in me even before I believed in myself. His belief in me for who I am has given me the confidence that propelled me forward. His support day in and day out has contributed greatly toward creating my deeply life and business. My gratitude to him goes beyond words. It is deep. It is truly heartfelt. It is precious.

I would like to thank all my teachers, coaches, and guides who greatly supported me in my journey and were there for me above and beyond their call of duty. I would like to especially acknowledge Marie-Danielle Boyer, Eden Clark, Doreen Mary Bray, the late Sanjay Nimar, teachers in my schools, CTI—The Coaches Training Institute, and The Four Winds Society.

I would like to thank my friends, and especially my Oriole leadership flock, who supported me and accepted me unconditionally. They saw my gifts and encouraged me to bring them forward.

I am truly grateful to my team who helped me make this book happen: Brandylane Publishers, Ceci Hughes, Erin Harpst, Erin Lariviere, Grace Albritton, Liz Lee, Nancy Morris, Shari Reinhart and Tarek Riman.

I would like to acknowledge Carolyn Flower, who inspired the title of this book.

A special thank you to my beautiful dog Coco, whose unconditional love and cuteness gave me the extra support I needed during late nights of working on my book.

Finally, I would like to thank the Universe for guiding and inspiring me every step of the way. It never let me down. Thank you, thank you, and thank you!!!

References

Professional Development Training

Access Consciousness® offers pragmatic tools to change things in your life that you haven't been able to change until now: www.access-consciousness.com.

Co-Active Training Institute, CTI®, is the largest in-person coach training school in the world and the only program to teach CTI's ground-breaking Co-active Coaching® model in highly interactive courses. CTI's proven whole-life coaching approach enables people to achieve success and fulfillment in their work and life through a powerful coach/client alliance that promotes and enhances the lifelong process of learning: www.coactive.com.

Professional Co-Active Leadership Training creates a new language of leadership that transforms businesses, organizations, and communities throughout the world: www.coactive.com/training/leadership-training.

The Four Winds Society offers the world's most thorough training in Shamanic Energy Medicine. Through the marriage of ancient wisdom and modern science, they seek to transform the world by bringing exceptional health and joy to everyone they work with: www.thefourwinds.com.

Works Cited

Alshami, Ali M. "Pain: Is It All in the Brain or the Heart?" *PubMed*, November 14, 2019. https://pubmed.ncbi.nlm.nih.gov/31728781/

The Arbinger Institute. *The Anatomy of Peace: Resolving the Heart of Conflict*. Oakland, CA: Berrett-Koehler Publishers, 2015.

Bernstein, Gabby. "Cut the Cord: Practice the Powerful Cord-Cutting Meditation." *gabbybernstein.com,* April 2, 2020. https://gabbybernstein.com/cut-the-cord/

Bonchek, Mark. "Why the Problem with Learning is Unlearning." *ShiftThinking*, Nov 3, 2016. https://www.shift.to/articles/2016/11/10/why-the-problem-with-learning-is-unlearning

Calbet, Josep. "Hebb's rule with an analogy." *Neuro Quotient*, March 14, 2018. https://neuroquotient.com/en/pshychology-and-neuroscience-hebb-principle-rule/

Callaway, Ewen. "Fearful Memories Passed Down to Mouse Descendants." *Scientific American*, Dec 1, 2013. https://www.scientificamerican.com/article/fearful-memories-passed-down/

Cloud, Henry. Necessary Endings: The Employees, Businesses, and Relationships That All of Us Have to Give Up in Order to Move Forward. New York: Harper Business, 2011.

Co-Active Training Institute. "What is Co-Active?" *coactive.com*, accessed September 29th, 2022. https://coactive.com/about/what-is-coactive/.

Collins, Jim. Good to Great: Why Some Companies Make the Leap and Others Don't. New York: HarperBusiness, 2001.

Costa, Dora, Noelle Yetter and Heather DeSomer. "Intergenerational transmission of paternal trauma among US Civil War ex-POWs." *The Proceedings of the National Academy of Sciences*, October 30, 2018. https://www.pnas.org/content/115/44/11215

Delahooke, Mona. Beyond Behaviors: Using Brain Science and Compassion to Understand and Solve Children's Behavioral

Challenges. Eau Claire, WI: PESI Publishing, 2019.

Dinner, M, dir. *Justified*. Season 4, episode 1, "Hole in the Wall." Aired January 8, 2013, on FX.

DiSalvo, David. "Your Brain Sees Even When You Don't." *Forbes*. June 22, 2013. https://www.forbes.com/sites/daviddisalvo/2013/06/22/your-brain-sees-even-when-you-dont/?sh=6544008c116a

Dispenza, Joe. Breaking the Habit of Being Yourself: How to Lose Your Mind and Create a New One. Carlsbad, CA: Hay House, 2013.

Johnson, Robert A. Owning Your Own Shadow: Understanding the Dark Side of the Psyche. New York: HarperOne, 2009.

Pagano, R R, and L R Frumkin. "The effect of transcendental meditation on right hemispheric functioning." *Biofeedback and self-regulation* vol. 2,4 (1977): 407-15. doi:10.1007/BF00998625

HeartMath. "Fascinating Relationship Between the Heart and Brain." HeartMath Institute, n.d. https://www.heartmath.org/resources/videos/heart-and-brain-relationship/

Heer, Dain. "How Does It Get Any Better?" *YouTube*, September 23, 2009. https://www.youtube.com/watch?v=1k-gH8CJ0NQ

Heer, Dain. "The Light And Heavy Tool with Dain Heer." *YouTube*, November 25, 2016. https://www.youtube.com/watch?v=_-5xeDr0RB4

Hemphill, Prentis. (n.d.) https://prentishemphill.com/blog

Karpman, Stephen. "Fairy tales and script drama analysis." *Transactional Analysis Bulletin*, 7,26, (1968): 39-43.

Kimsey-House, Henry, and Karen Kimsey-House. *Co-Active Leadership: Five Ways to Lead*. Oakland, CA: Berrett-Koehler Publishers, 2015.

Kondo, Marie. The Life-Changing Magic of Tidying Up: The Japanese Art of Decluttering and Organizing. Berkeley, CA: Ten Speed Press, 2014.

Lancer, Darlene. "Price and Payoff of a Gray Rock Strategy." *Psychology Today*, November 4, 2019. https://www.psychologytoday.com/us/blog/toxic-relationships/201911/the-price-and-payoff-gray-rock-strategy

Landry, Andrea. "How I'm raising my daughter to be 100 percent, unapologetically Indigenous." *Today's Parent*, May 22, 2021. https://www.todaysparent.com/family/parenting/how-im-raising-my-daughter-to-be-100-percent-unapologetically-indigenous/

Bunston, Wendy and Sarah Jones, eds. Supporting Vulnerable Babies and Young Children: Interventions for Working with Trauma, Mental Health, Illness and Other Complex Challenges. London: Jessica Kingsley Publishers, 2019.

The Norwegian University of Science and Technology (NTNU). "Brain Waves and Meditation." *ScienceDaily*, March 31, 2010.

Rivera, Luis Soler. "Effects of Sugar on the Brain: Cravings and Inflammation." *UVAHealth*, January 15, 2020. https://blog.uvahealth.com/2020/01/15/effects-sugar-brain/

Robertson, Ruairi. "The Gut-Brain Connection: How it Works and The Role of Nutrition." *Healthline*, August 20, 2020. https://www.healthline.com/nutrition/gut-brain-connection#TOC_TITLE_HDR_2

Selhub, Eva. "Nutritional Psychiatry: Your brain on food." *Harvard Health Blog*, March 26, 2020. https://www.health.harvard.edu/blog/nutritional-psychiatry-your-brain-on-food-201511168626

Shepherd, Phillip. Radical Wholeness: The Embodied Present and the Ordinary Grace of Being. Berkeley, CA: North Atlantic Books, 2017.

Siegel, Ethan. "You Are Not Mostly Empty Space." *Forbes*, April 16, 2020. https://www.forbes.com/sites/startswithabang/2020/04/16/you-are-not-mostly-empty-space/?sh=69225152c2b0

Underwood, Emily. "Your gut is directly connected to your brain, by a newly discovered neuron circuit." *Science*, September 20, 2018. https://www.science.org/content/article/your-gut-directly-connected-your-brain-newly-discovered-neuron-circuit

Villoldo, Alberto. Grow a New Body: How Spirit and Power Plant Nutrients Can Transform Your Health. Carlsbad, CA: Hay House, 2019.

Emspak, J. "Quantum entanglement: A simple explanation." *Space*, March 16, 2022. https://www.space.com/31933-quantum-entanglement-action-at-a-distance.html

Wolfe, Laurie. "How Meditation Changes Your Brain." *The Expanding Light*, July 26, 2014. https://www.expandinglight.org/blog/meditation/meditation-teacher-training/how-meditation-changes-your-brain/

Recommended Reading:

Cloud, Henry and John Townsend. Boundaries: When to Say Yes, How to Say No to Take Control of Your Life. Grand Rapids, MI: Zondervan, 1992.

Cloud, Henry and John Townsend. How to Have That Difficult Conversation: Gaining the Skills for Honest and Meaningful Communication. Grand Rapids, MI: Zondervan, 2015.

Frankl, Viktor. *Man's Search for Meaning*. Boston, MA: Beacon Press, 1946.

Gibran, Kahlil. *The Prophet*. New York: Alfred A. Knopf, 1923.

GoZen. "A Better Way to Teach Kids About Emotions." GoZen, Sept 8, 2016. https://gozen.com/a-better-way-to-teach-kids-about-emotions/

HeartMath LLC. "Let Your Heart Talk to Your Brain." *Huffington Post,* Dec 6, 2017. https://www.huffpost.com/entry/heart-wisdom_b_2615857

HeartMath LLC. "The Mysteries of the Heart Infographic." *Heartmath. org,* n.d. https://www.heartmath.org/resources/infographic/mysteries-of-the-heart/

Heer, Dain. "The 'Who Does This Belong To App' introduced by Dr Dain Heer." *drdainheer.com*, October 30, 2016. http://drdainheer.com/whodoesthisbelongto/

Herold, Cameron. Vivid Vision: A Remarkable Tool for Aligning Your Business Around a Shared Vision of the Future. Austin, TX: Lioncrest Publishing, 2018.

Johnson, Robert A. Owning Your Own Shadow: Understanding the Dark Side of the Psyche. New York: HarperOne, 2009.

Kimsey-House, Henry, Karen Kimsey-House, Phillip Sandahl,and Laura Whitworth. *Co-Active Coaching: Changing Business, Transforming Lives*. Boston, MA: Nicholas Brealy Publishing, 2011.

Kofman, Fred. "Shifting from Unilateral Control to Mutual Learning."

Axialent Conscious Business, 2010. https://ap.uci.edu/wp-content/uploads/Shifting_from_Unilateral_Control_to_Mutual_Learning_by_Fred_Kofman1.pdf

Kofman, Fred. Conscious Business: How to Build Value Through Values. Boulder, CO: Sounds True, 2013.

Kimhealth (username). "Old cliché Or Powerful Detoxifier?" *Nutrition L'Écuyer*, Feb 15, 2021. https://www.nutritionlecuyer.ca/2021/02/old-cliche-or-powerful-detoxifier/

Lockett, Eleesha. "Grounding: Exploring Earthing Science and the Benefits Behind It." *Healthline*, August 30, 2019. https://www.healthline.com/health/grounding

Mayo Clinic Staff. "Meditation: Take a stress-reduction break wherever you are." *Mayo Clinic*, April 22, 2020. https://www.mayoclinic.org/tests-procedures/meditation/in-depth/meditation/art-20045858

McLeod, Saul. "Maslow's Hierarchy of Needs." *Simply Psychology*, December 29, 2020. https://www.simplypsychology.org/maslow.html

Miller, Meredith. "A Guide for Self-healing After Narcissistic Abuse | THE JOURNEY by Meredith Miller." *YouTube*, December 11, 2017. https://www.youtube.com/watch?v=eNWFuA_oZFM

Palo Santo Sticks. (n.d.) Retrieved from https://www.mountainroseherbs.com/products/palo-santo-smudge-sticks/profile

Dibdin, Emma. "The Health Benefits of Journaling." *PsychCentral*, March 30, 2022. https://psychcentral.com/lib/the-health-benefits-of-journaling

Villoldo, Alberto. The Heart of the Shaman: Stories and Practices of the Luminous Warrior. Carlsbad, CA: Hay House, 2018.

Williamson, Marianne. A Return to Love: Reflections on the Principles of "A Course in Miracles." New York: HarperOne, 1996.

Wolynn, Mark. It Didn't Start With You: How Inherited Family Trauma Shapes Who We Are and How to End the Cycle. New York: Penguin Books, 2017.

World Narcissistic Abuse Awareness Day. Retrieved from https://wnaad.com/

Zetlin, Minda. "Why You Need to Be Your Real Self at Work." *Inc.*, March 18, 2014. https://www.inc.com/minda-zetlin/why-you-need-to-put-your-real-self-in-your-professional-image.html

About the Author

Melissa Dawn is the founder of CEO of Your Life, a renowned speaker, author, executive leadership and conscious business coach, and master practitioner of energy medicine.

Melissa's life once looked picture perfect. But it was all a mask. Raised in a strictly religious community, where she was always watched, reported on, and brought back in line, Melissa lived a life where love always came with conditions and uniqueness was something to be stamped out. Through it all, she was pulled further and further away from her true self, as she was pushed to fit into a mold of "perfection."

It took a lot for Melissa to start seeing her world for what it was, removing her masks—one by one, confronting her fears, accepting the loss of family and community, and discovering the deep and powerful strength within her.

Today, Melissa guides others to drop their masks, reconnect with their core selves, and put themselves firmly in the CEO seat of their own lives. She believes that what makes us different is how we bring the greatest value to the world and ourselves.

Melissa is a Master Certified Coach (MCC), Certified Professional Co-Active Coach (CPCC), Certified Team Performance Coach (CTPC), Conscious Business Coach, and Certified Master Practitioner of Energy Medicine with The Four Winds. She holds a Bachelor of Commerce. She is a contributor to Thrive Global, *The Huffington Post*, and Entrepreneur.com and has been featured on many podcasts, radio, and television programs including *Entrepreneur on Fire*, *Breakfast Television*, Global News, CJAD Radio, the *Edmonton Journal*, and more. She is also the bestselling author of *I Attract What I Am: Transform Failure into an Orgasmically Joyful Life and Business* and was named one of Hubspot's Best Coaching Services worldwide for the past five years.

About the Illustrator

Liz Lee is a bilingual Montreal-based illustrator and graphic designer, foodie, and professional geek. She enjoys writing, creating comics, sustainable living, and exploring themes of mental health, environmental activism, and LGBTQIA+ issues in her artwork. She can be found slurping on oat milk lattes and talking aloud to her dog Misha as she haunts local cafes to do her contract work.

www.ingramcontent.com/pod-product-compliance
Lightning Source LLC
Chambersburg PA
CBHW072139090426
42739CB00013B/3228